Truth, Testimony, and Transformation

Truth, Testimony, and Transformation

A New Reading of the
"I Am" Sayings of Jesus
in the Fourth Gospel

YUNG SUK KIM

CASCADE *Books* • Eugene, Oregon

TRUTH, TESTIMONY, AND TRANSFORMATION
A New Reading of the "I Am" Sayings of Jesus in the Fourth Gospel

Cascade Books
An Imprint of Wipf and Stock Publishers
199 W. 8th Ave., Suite 3
Eugene, OR 97401

www.wipfandstock.com

ISBN 13: 978-1-62032-222-2

Cataloging-in-Publication data:

Kim, Yung Suk

    Truth, testimony, and transmission : a new reading of the "I-am" sayings of Jesus in the fourth gospel / Yung Suk Kim.

    xii + 90 p. ; 23 cm. —Includes bibliographical references and index(es).

    ISBN 13: 978-1-62032-222-2

1. Bible. John—Criticism, interpretation, etc. I. Title.

BS2615.52 K569 2014

Manufactured in the U.S.A.

To Larry Welborn, my mentor and colleague

If you remain faithful to my teaching, you are truly my disciples; and you will know the truth, and the truth will make you free

(JOHN 8:31–32)

I am the way, the truth, and the life. No one comes to the Father except through me

(JOHN 14:6)

Sanctify them in the truth; your word is truth. As you have sent me into the world, so I have sent them into the world

(JOHN 17:17–18)

I was born and came into the world for this reason: to testify to the truth. Whoever accepts the truth listens to my voice

(JOHN 18:37)

Contents

Preface

When Jesus says in the Fourth Gospel, "I am the way, the truth, and the life," does he mean that Christianity is the only true religion, or did he mean something else? As we know, Jesus did not found a new religion nor did he pave a new way to salvation or truth. Rather, Jesus worked for God, by showing the way of God, testifying to the truth, and engaging in the work of liberation. Jesus in the Fourth Gospel, like Moses, is sent by God to liberate people from darkness. Unlike today's triumphant Christianity, the Johannine community was a small, marginalized, expelled community that struggled because of their faith. It will be very interesting to see how this struggling community was transformed into a loving community, following the model of Jesus.

I wrote this book out of my hope that the Fourth Gospel and John 14:6 in particular could be the scripture of engagement, embodiment, and empowerment for Christian readers. I hope this book will help the reader rethink the role of the Logos or the "I am" sayings in the Fourth Gospel. In a pluralistic society, the focus of the gospel shifts from conversion or theological doctrine to empowerment of people. I dream that this book will contribute to theological education in that the "I am" sayings of the Fourth Gospel give a voice of inclusivism rather than exclusivism, solidarity rather than marginalization, and liberation rather than oppression. In the pluralistic life contexts of America today, the theology that accepts others as friends is very important; it engages others on the basis of God's love and justice. With a focus on the language of embodiment and empowerment, theological education can be more inclusive to others and help students to reorient their attention to the present life in the world.

More importantly, by extending the horizons of biblical theology to aspects of psychological theology and political theology, theological education can be more holistic and fruitful.

Likewise, I hope this book will inform the life of the church so that Christians can be ethically more sensitive to others and/or other views of life by focusing on Jesus' embodiment. Other religious people should not be the target of the Christian mission but partners in dialogue through mutual challenge and encouragement because of the divine presence in the world. As a result, Christian life or discipleship is more focused on the embodiment of the divine presence manifest in Jesus.

Certainly, I hope this book will develop a greater public voice for theology in society in that a just, livable, lovable society is more important than the mere theology of divine identity. Understood in this way, Christian theology is not different from Christian ethics because theology can engage in the real world. This congruence of theology and ethics is possible because the "I am" sayings are Jesus' embodiment of God's love at all costs. That is how the Johannine Christians understood the Logos and applied it to their lives. This idea offers new perspectives on Christianity in a pluralistic setting because now the "I am" sayings are no longer exclusive; rather, they may serve as a stimulus for interracial, intercultural, and interreligious dialogue. As Jesus embodied the divine presence through the "I am" saying of God, Christians need to embody the "I am" sayings of Jesus. When this happens, there is a true dialogue, mutual understanding, and ethical sensitivity to others. The more important thing is not a mere personal identity but an actual living of the Logos. This means that belief in Jesus is not enough. Accepting Jesus as the Logos incarnate means risking one's life; only then, Christians are given the power of becoming the children of God (John 1:12).

Acknowledgments

N ow sitting back in my office, I take joy in pondering on the people whom I have to thank and acknowledge. First of all, I give thanks to Stephen Graham, Director of Faculty Development, and Frances Pacienza, of Association of Theological Schools, who were quick to help process my application for the Lilly Theological Scholars Grant. I am very grateful for this grant by which my research has been done without worries. I also thank my peers and friends at the ATS conference of grant recipients who gave me solid feedback on my research project. I also give special thanks to Larry Welborn, Professor of New Testament at Fordham University, who strongly supported my research by writing a strong letter of recommendation for the grant and encouraged me to pursue the project with confidence. I won't forget our pleasant conversations about this book and other topics at his place in Dayton, Ohio in the summer of 2012. In addition, I would like to give special thanks to Jon Berquist, president of Disciples Seminary Foundation, who wholeheartedly supported my research project, especially in my application for the Lilly grant.

I also give special thanks to R. Alan Culpepper, dean of Mercer Divinity School, who spent time with me at his office when I sought his input concerning my research project. He was very gentle and helpful to all of my questions. He provided me with copies of and a list of his works, which have been very informative and helpful to my ongoing research. My work represents the spirit of his genuine, critical, faithful scholarship. I also have to mention Paul Anderson, Professor of Biblical and Quaker Studies at George Fox University, who provided me with his recent articles and encouraging words. His approach to the Fourth Gospel was the matter on which this book is based. I thank him for his pioneering scholarship.

I am so thankful for the support and understanding of my research project by my dean, John Kinney. Because of his understanding, I could focus on my research and teaching. I also thank my colleagues and staff in the School of Theology for their caring spirit and speedy work on my behalf. I love my students who kept an open mind in order to engage in class. I taught John's Gospel three times in a row and I learned a lot from my students.

I cannot emphasize enough my family's love and sacrifice for me. My wife, Yong-Jeong, is an amazing and intellectual woman who always supports my work and humanity as it is. I love all of my three daughters, each of whom is dear to me: Hye Rim, Hye Kyung, and Hye In. I cannot fail to mention Hye Kyung's brilliant mind, as she has read part of this manuscript with some helpful input to me.

1

Introduction

This book challenges the high Christology of Jesus in the Fourth
Gospel[1] and argues that Jesus is best understood as the Jewish
Messiah (low Christology), who is sent by, and working for, God.[2]
Jesus as the Son of God[3] shows God the Father to the world by

1. Robert Kysar states that there are three concepts of Christ in the New Tes-
tament: "adoptionistic," "agency," and "incarnational." The adoptionistic Chris-
tology is found in the Gospel of Matthew; Jesus is adopted as God's Messiah
because of his obedience to God. Agency Christology, widespread in the New
Testament, means that Jesus is sent by God to serve God, doing the work of
God as the Son of God. Incarnational Christology in the Fourth Gospel means
Jesus is God incarnate; Jesus is God. See Kysar, *John the Maverick Gospel*, 33–34.
But this division of three christological concepts is not apparent. For example,
Matthew's Gospel has all three concepts: adoption (Jesus is the adopted Son
of God at his baptism); agency (obeying the will of God as the Son of God);
and incarnation (doing the work of God through his life and death). Likewise,
all three concepts appear in Romans 1:3–6: adoption ("descended from David
according to the flesh"); agency ("declared to be the Son of God"); incarnation
("according to the spirit of holiness").

2. Anderson argues that Jesus in the Fourth Gospel is "radically Jewish." See
Anderson, *The Riddles of the Fourth Gospel*, 15.

3. In the Hebrew Bible the "Son of God" refers to Israel (Exod 4:22; Hos
11:1; Jer 31:20), to the Israelites (Hos 2:1; Isa 1:2; Jer 3:19), or to the leaders of
the people such as kings, princes, and judges (Isa 9:5; Ps 2:7; 89:27; 110:3). In
the Fourth Gospel, the "Son of Man" is used with a focus on Jesus' humanity;
Jesus lays down his life to embody God's love in the world (John 1:51; 3:13–14;
5:27; 6:27, 53; 8:28; 12:23, 34).

discerning the way of God, testifying to the truth, and liberating people from darkness in the world. That is why Jesus says in John 14:6: "I am the way, and the truth, and the life; no one comes to the Father except through me."[4] Jesus incarnates the Logos of God[5] through his life and death. Likewise, the "I am" sayings of Jesus can be understood as Jesus' enactment of the Logos of God rather than as "Jesus' divine self-revelation."[6]

In fact, low Christology is well attested throughout the Fourth Gospel. First, Jesus never says he is God.[7] His self-understanding

4. There are seven "I am" sayings of Jesus in the Fourth Gospel, which are symbolic or metaphoric: "I am the bread of life" (6:35, 48); "I am the light of the world" (8:12); "I am the gate of the sheep" (10:9); "I am the good shepherd" (10:11, 14); "I am the resurrection and the life" (11:25); "I am the way, the truth, and the life. No one comes to the Father except through me" (14:6); and "I am the true vine" (15:1).

5. As will be argued in this book, the Logos in the Fourth Gospel is understood in terms of God's Logos that Jesus embodies. With clues from Genesis 1 and throughout the Hebrew Scriptures, the Logos of God connotes at least the following: God's word, God's Spirit, God's wisdom, and God's creative and redemptive power. The Logos in the prologue of the Fourth Gospel is clearly God's Logos that Jesus incarnates: "The Logos became flesh" (John 1:14). More strikingly, the Logos in John 1:1 ("In the beginning was the Logos, and the Logos was with God, and the Logos was God") echoes Gen 1:1–2: "In the beginning when God created the heavens and the earth . . . the Spirit of God (or a wind from God) swept over the face of the water." The Logos in John is God's, not Jesus.' When Jesus prays to God, he refers to God's Logos: "Your word (Logos) is truth" (John 17:17; see also 17:14). Therefore, the idea of Jesus as the preexistent Logos is hardly found in the prologue or throughout the Gospel. Therefore, it is very important to distinguish God's Logos from Jesus because the former is carried out by the latter, who is the Jewish Messiah. In other words, he is best understood from a low christological perspective.

6. Satoko Yamaguchi summarizes two typical ways of reading the "I am" sayings of Jesus in the Fourth Gospel: "Jesus' divine self-revelation" and "Jesus as not revealing himself, but as revealing the God." See Yamaguchi, "'I Am' Sayings and Women in Context," 35–40. Rudolf Bultmann takes the former reading: "I am" sayings as "the existential embodiment." See Bultmann, *The Theology of the New Testament*, 2:64–66; Bultmann, *The Gospel of John*, 327n5. See also Ball, "'My Lord and my God': The Implication of 'I Am' sayings for Religious Pluralism," 53–71. See Kysar, *John the Maverick Gospel*, 27–28; Dodd, *The Interpretation of the Fourth Gospel*, 93–96; Brown, *The Gospel According to John*, 86–88, 533–38; Barrett, *Essays on John*, 1–18; and Robinson, *The Priority of John*, 387.

7. Jesus is not worshipped as a God in the New Testament in general. Two different verbs, *proskuneo* and *latreuo*, are often translated into "to worship"

is the Son of God,[8] and he refutes Jews' claim that he is equal with God: "So how can you say that the one whom the Father has made holy and sent into the world insults God because he said, 'I am God's Son'?" (John 10:36). Here Jesus quotes from Psalm 82:6 and argues that the Son of God is not a God, and that even some people are called gods not because they are gods but because they are leaders of the people (John 10:34). It is an irony that Jews accuse Jesus of blasphemy, because in Jewish tradition the Son of God is not divine or equal with God. The "Son of God" refers to Israel (Exod 4:22; Hos 11:1; Jer 31:20), to the Israelites (Hos 2:1; Isa 1:2; Jer 3:19), or to the leaders of the people such as kings, princes, and judges (Isa 9:5; Ps 2:7; 89:27; 110:3). In fact, Jesus says that the Father is greater than he (John 14:28). Similarly, he says: "Servants are not greater than their master" (John 13:16). Even when he talks about the unity of him and the Father: "I and the Father are one" (John 10:30), it does not mean that Jesus and God are equal and the same.[9] Actually, "one" is a neuter noun (*hen*), which connotes the relationship of unity rather than that of equality. If the masculine form (*heis*) was used, it could mean the equality between God and Jesus. But throughout the Gospel Jesus always says that he is working for God the Father who sent him. Jesus' identity as the Son of God would be hollow apart from his works of God. Jesus says, "If I don't do the works of my Father, don't believe

---

without distinction. But they are not the same. The former, *prokuneo*, means giving honor or respect to divine or human beings (for example: Matt 4:10; 18:26; 20:20; Rev 9:20, etc.). See the *Greek-English Lexicon*, 882–83.The latter, *latreuo*, however, is primarily used for deities in a worship or cultic setting (for example: Matt 4:10; Luke 4:8; Act 7:7; 24:14; 27:23; Heb 9:14; Rev 7:15; 22:3). See the *Greek-English Lexicon*, 587. See also Dunn, *Did the First Christians Worship Jesus?*, 7–28.

8. Jesus refers to himself as the Son of God when he raises Lazarus (11:4). Also, he defends his work as the Son of God whose job is to do work for God (10:34–36). John the Baptist also testifies about Jesus and calls him the Son of God (1:34). Nathanael also says: "Rabbi, you are the Son of God! You are the King of Israel!" (1:49). Martha also addresses Jesus as the Son of God, the Messiah (11:27). Jews also accuse Jesus because he claimed he is the Son of God (19:7). About the Son of God in the Roman world, see Peppard, *The Son of God in the Roman World*, 31–49.

9. Similarly, if I say to my children that "we are one," it does not mean that my children and I are the same in any sense, but it means we are united in terms of love and care.

me. But if I do them, and you don't believe me, believe the works so that you can know and recognize that the Father is in me and I am in the Father" (John 10:37–38; *Common English Bible*).

Second, Jesus in the Fourth Gospel is more comparable to Moses than to God. As Moses is called by God to deliver the Israelites from the bondage of slavery in Egypt (Exod 3:1–21; 7:1), so is Jesus sent by God to deliver God's people from darkness.[10] Moses is sent like God for God's work ("I have made you like God to Pharaoh," Exod 7:1); similarly, Jesus is sent by God as the Son of God who does the work of God. The only difference is the object of mission. Moses is called for Israelites; Jesus is called for the whole world[11]: "God so loved the world that he gave his only Son . . . God sent the Son into the world, not to condemn the world, but that the world might be saved through him" (John 3:16–17).

Third, Jesus' "I am" sayings are not meant to say he is divine. When Jesus says, "I am" (*ego eimi*) to the trembling disciples while walking on the water (John 6:16–21), he means not that he is a God but that "It's me, Jesus! Do not fear because God will protect you."[12] In such a situation of the sweeping storms, Jesus comforts them with his presence as the Son of God ("I am"), assuring them that God's love is enough. In this context, the "I am" sayings of Jesus can be best understood as his embodiment of God's presence in the world. That is, Jesus shows the way of God through his life and death. It is not a new way or another way but the way of God found in Isa 40:3, "Make straight the way of the Lord," which John the Baptist cites and proclaims in the wilderness (John 1:23). Jesus continues the way of God, as John the Baptist prepares. As we will explore, Jesus discerns the way of God and lives with it. His way is narrow, not a paved highway to success but the way of the cross through which all people may be led to the kingdom of God (in the sense of God's rule). This way

10. Anderson, *The Riddles of the Fourth Gospel*, 131–33.

11. In Johannine language, the world (*cosmos*) is a double entendre: the world as the object of God's love (John 3:16–17); the world as a hostile force that resists the Logos of God and Jesus (John 1:10–12).

12. "I am" (*ego eimi*) in John 6:16–21 and 8:58 is often associated with *ehyeh asher ehyeh* ("I shall be that I shall be") in Exod 3:14. Though the Septuagint translates it as "I am the one who exists" (*eimi ho on*) to show that God is permanent, the Hebrew text hardly means such an ontological sense influenced by Hellenistic philosophy. We will explore this in the next chapter.

is the way on which Jesus invites his disciples to join him. This way continues to be trodden by his disciples. This understanding of Jesus being the way ("I am the way") differs from that of Jesus being the accomplished, paved way because of his atoning sacrifice, through which all people can get on the right way to God or heaven.

Fourth, Jesus is not merely the object of faith; his own faithfulness to God must be highlighted. His voluntary, sacrificial love for God and the world cannot be forgotten. Jesus' faithfulness is expressed through his mission of the Logos: "The Logos that you hear is not mine, but is from the Father who sent me" (John 14:24b). Furthermore, when Jesus prays to the Father, he says: "I gave *your Logos* to them and the world hated them" (John 17:14). Jesus goes on to pray to the Father: "Make them holy in the truth; *your Logos* is truth" (John 17:17).[13] The Logos of God here is essentially not different from the Logos in the prologue, in which the Logos was with God and was God.

Fifth, Jesus does not come to die in place of sinners in the way of a vicarious death or in the sense of a penal substitution. Forgiveness occurs through mutual forgiving in the Fourth Gospel: "If you forgive anyone's sins, they are forgiven" (John 20:23). The concept of sin in this Gospel is "not a moral category of behavior but a theological category about one's responsibility to the revelation of God in Jesus."[14] Interestingly, it is Caiaphas the high priest who has the

13. Truth (*emet*) in the Hebrew Bible has to do with "a root meaning reliable, steadfast, and faithful." See Hazony, *The Philosophy of Hebrew Scripture*, 198. God is true because he is reliable, steadfast, and faithful. Jesus speaks for God and acts out of God's character of truth. As Hazony argues, the concept of truth in the Hebrew Bible is very different from Aristotle's *Metaphysics* that reads: "To say of what is that is not, or of what is not that it is, is false; while to say of what is that it is, and of what is not that it is not, is true" (Aristotle, *Metaphysics* 1011b25). Whereas Aristotle emphasizes a metaphysical, ontological fact of things (e.g., the truth is that a cat is not a mouse), the Hebrew Bible emphasizes "an act of truth," as Hazony put it: "Truth can be a quality of an action if it is understood as evincing reliability, steadfastness, or faithfulness. In this, the truth of an action that is done to or for someone, or the truth of an action when it is performed "in truth," can be seen to differ in no essential respect from the truth that is a quality of objects" (200). So the Logos of God is true (John 17:17) because God's character and act is reliable, steadfast, and faithful. Jesus testifies to the truth by his faithful living of God's Logos.

14. O'Day, "John," 1947. In fact, sin in the Fourth Gospel is "singular and emphasizes the world's collective alienation from God and one another, rather

notion of a vicarious death of Jesus and advises "the Jews that it was better to have one person die for the people" (John 18:14). However, the Fourth Gospel does not present Jesus' death as atonement for sins or for particular people. Jesus' death is the result of the costly life of the Logos mission. If Jesus' mission of the Logos had been accepted in the world, he would not have ended up on a cross. Jesus' death is not the end for or by itself. Even when Jesus says his last words on the cross—"It is finished" (John 19:30)—it does not mean that his death completed all salvific works, once and for all. Rather, it should mean plainly that he has done the work of God that he was supposed to do, which is to embody the Logos of God (4:34; 5:36; 17:4).

Sixth, "believing in Jesus" is more than a belief in Jesus. Translating the verb *pisteuo* as "to believe" is evasive.[15] The problem is, there are few adequate English verbs for *pisteuo* other than "to believe," which derives from the noun "belief." We wish to have the imaginative verb like "faithize" for the verb *pisteuo*.[16] While the noun *pistis* is translated as faith, *pisteuo* does not have a similar "faith" cognate. This creates a huge problem for many readers because the dynamic nature of faith is not conveyed through the verb "to believe." In Jewish scriptures and tradition, faith means trust in God—a life of faithfulness for God. New Testament writers in general, except for

---

than a catalog of human sin," as we see in John 1:29: "Here is the Lamb of God who takes away the sin of the world." Sin is not to know God and to dwell in darkness, to live a life apart from God (John 15:21–25). O'Day, "John," 1909.

15. Kim, *A Theological Introduction to Paul's Letters*, 64.

16. Typically, the verb *pisteuo* is followed by a few different prepositions: *eis* (toward or into), *en* (in), and *epi* (on). The *eis* is used with a person as the object. For example, *pisteuo eis Christon* means "I trust in Christ" in the sense that "I participate in Christ." The *en* is used with a non-personal object such as the "good news": "Believe in the good news" (Mark 1:15). Therefore, if *pisteuo* followed by *eis* is used for a person, we had better translate it as "to trust" rather than "to believe" so that we may distinguish the two different prepositions (*eis* and *en*). On the other hand, when *pisteuo* is used with the preposition *epi* ("upon" or "on the basis of" if used with a dative), which appears in 1 Tim 1:16 ("believe in him for eternal life"), the emphasis here is that the believer has to believe something about Jesus. This view of faith is consistent in the Pastoral Letters, where faith generally means what to believe (1 Tim 1:3–5, 13–14; 4:6; 2 Tim. 3:15). This later usage of faith is very different from Paul's undisputed letters or the canonical Gospels.

maybe those of the deutero-Pauline and Pastoral letters, follow this tradition of faith.[17]

In this context, believing in Jesus means following his teaching.[18] So Jesus says, "If you continue in my word, you are truly my disciples; and you will know the truth, and the truth will make you free'" (John 8:31–32). Thus believing in Jesus is about true discipleship that is based on constant abiding in Jesus' word.[19] True disciples will know (future tense) the truth, which suggests that the truth is not possessed in the present, but visible or experiential in the future. Then they will be free (future tense). Freedom is not obtained once and for all since it is not possessive; it is not granted through belief in Jesus but through living the truth of God through the example of Jesus.

OVERVIEW OF JOHANNINE SCHOLARSHIP[20]

A first approach to the Fourth Gospel is a *harmonious theological reading*, like a personal devotional reading of the Bible, in which the message of the Fourth Gospel is not different from the Synoptic Gospels.[21] Differences among the gospels are either downplayed or justified. For example, the absence of the water baptism in the Fourth

17. See Kim, *A Theological Introduction to Paul's Letters*, 63–82.

18. Interestingly, Paul's seven undisputed letters have a similar view of Christology or theology in the sense that Christ's faith (*pistis christou*) is needed to manifest God's righteousness (*dikaiosyne theou*) and becomes a model for believers. See Kim, *A Theological Introduction to Paul's Letters*, 15–37.

19. Whitters, "Discipleship in John: Four Profiles," 422–27.

20. Since the Fourth Gospel involves a rich history of interpretation, it is virtually impossible to give a fair, extensive review of scholarly literature in this small volume. For an overview of Johannine scholarship, see Anderson, *The Riddles of the Fourth Gospel*, 95–124. Instead of a full review, I will briefly consider various approaches to the Fourth Gospel and discuss their pros and cons.

21. Regarding the traditional view about the author of the Fourth Gospel, see Anderson, *The Riddles of the Fourth Gospel*, 96–99. According to William Temple, the differences between them are matters of focus or style of Jesus' teaching. For example, while the Synoptic Gospels contain the public ministry and teaching of Jesus, the Gospel of John has more of Jesus' intimate, private teachings to his disciples. See Temple, *Readings in St. John's Gospel*. xxii–xxxii. This kind of a harmonious approach is usually done in church bible study. For example, see Matson, *John*, 2–3.

Truth, Testimony, and Transformation

Gospel is because the baptism of the Holy Spirit is more important than water baptism. In this way, the absence of water baptism in the Fourth Gospel is not evidence that there was no water baptism in the Johannine community, or that water baptism is inconsequential. The absence of something does not corroborate nonexistence of a certain practice. The other example of a harmonious reading in the Fourth Gospel is seen in the discrepancy on the day of Jesus' death. Whereas Jesus dies after the Passover meal in the Synoptic Gospels, in the Fourth Gospel he dies on the day of preparation for the Passover. Either of them may be correct or both of them incorrect; but both of them cannot be correct. But in this harmonious theological approach, it may be argued that there were multiple versions of the calendar used at that time, and so the date of Jesus' death is the same with all four gospels. One last example regards the cause or meaning of Jesus' death. A vicarious death of Jesus is presupposed in this reading. But this forced theological harmony does a disservice to the distinctive theological features of each gospel. In reading this way, the particular issues faced by the Johannine community are not dealt with properly, and the role of Jesus as the Jewish Messiah is nonexistent.

A second approach to the Fourth Gospel features a distinct *spiritual gospel.*[22] The key is the relationship with God through the Son or the Spirit. The style or language of the Gospel is cosmic or existential.[23] Within this approach there are two different tracks: one with the more traditional side of the spiritual gospel that emphasizes a personal spiritual relationship with God, and the other one with the more inclusive side of the spiritual gospel that includes the spiritual union of the church and the world.[24] Overall, this distinct spiritual

22. Clement of Alexandria called the Fourth Gospel "a spiritual gospel." Eusebius, *Hist. Eccl.* 6.14.6. Because of this kind of spiritual language in the Fourth Gospel, Rudolf Bultmann thinks that the Fourth Gospel features a gnosticizing movement and that "I am" sayings are to be understood as part of such a movement in the Johannine community. See Bultmann, "The History of Religions Background of the prologue to the Gospel of John," 27–46. See also Smith, *The Composition and Order of the Fourth Gospel*, 15–34.

23. For example, see Bultmann, *Theology of the New Testament*, 2:15–92.

24. Petros Vassiliadis's reading of the Fourth Gospel represents the latter reading of this spiritual gospel; Eucharist (John 6) is a decisive moment of unity that binds people of the church. See Vassiliadis, "John in an Orthodox

8

gospel tradition highlights relational language through which the sense of personal identity is emphasized. However, on the flip side, there is no emphasis on the transformation of the world or society.

A third approach to the Fourth Gospel is a *sociological or social-scientific* reading.[25] One premise in this approach is that the Fourth Gospel is distinct from the Synoptic Gospels because it does not have common sources. The other premise is that the Fourth Gospel reflects the Johannine community's particular context of separation and expulsion from the synagogue (9:22; 12:42). In this approach, the Johannine community is seen as a sectarian community that strives to survive and grow even under pressure or separation from mainline Judaism. A sociological reading sheds new light on our understanding of this distinct community struggling with its identity or faith because of recent conflict with the synagogue. There are many benefits to this approach. For example, we learn that the Johannine community and its members are in conflict with the mainline community (the synagogue) because of their new faith that Christ Jesus is the Jewish Messiah. We also know that humans are social beings that need protection and survival in times of crisis. But the weakness of this reading is that there is no exploration of the possible transformation that the community undergoes, beyond the logic of "either/or," or "us and them." There is no room for engaging the world through the love of God for the whole world.

A fourth approach to the Fourth Gospel reflects the latest scholarly activity, as seen in the "John, Jesus, and History Group" at the Society of Biblical Literature.[26] The whole point in this approach is that the Fourth Gospel is close to the center of the *historical Jesus or early Christian tradition*, and that it shares major theological points with the Synoptic Gospels.[27] Among others, Louis Martyn stands out

---

Perspective," 412–18.

25. For example, see Meeks, "The Man from Heaven in Johannine Sectarianism," 44–72.

26. http://johannine.org/JJH.html (accessed September 24, 2011).

27. One indication that the Fourth Gospel has an early Jewish basis is that it contains unique Jewish or Aramaic terms that are translated into Greek for non-Jewish audiences: Rabbi (1:38); *messias* (1:41; 4:25); Kephas (1:42); Golgotha (19:17); and Rabbouni (20:16). For detailed argument, see Anderson, *The Riddles of the Fourth Gospel*, 62–65; 125–55. Anderson argues that there are two independent gospel traditions derived from the earliest Jesus tradition: Mark

in his research, which puts the Fourth Gospel back in the context of Jesus and the Johannine community.[28] According to Martyn, the Fourth Gospel contains a two-level conflict drama with Jesus and the Johannine community: the story of Jesus' conflict with Jews and the story of the Johannine community's conflict with the synagogue in the late first century (80–90s).[29] Given the current scholarship in the Fourth Gospel, this book's approach is close to the fourth approach.

METHODS

To begin with, distinction should be made between literalism and literal reading. The latter is a neutral term, derived from the Latin *sensus literalis*, "meaning according to the letter." In this sense of *literal* reading, all readings are literal. But the *literalist* reading ignores a deeper symbolic or metaphorical sense. Moreover, it ignores even the great tradition developed during medieval time, the so-called fourfold sense of the text: literal or historical, tropological (moral), allegorical, and anagogical (ultimate or eschatological).[30] As an example of strict literalism, we may consider Jesus' origin or the idea of incarnation theology in the prologue of John (1:1–18). The Logos becoming flesh (John 1:14) is not to be read as literalistic but as incarnational theology in the way that God's presence is manifest through the life and death of Jesus. The meaning here is not that God became Jesus quite literally. Similarly, when Jesus says that he is the living bread coming from God, and asks people to eat his flesh and drink his blood, he does not mean that his flesh is the bread. The living bread as a metaphor quite likely means "life." Ironically, people, even within the stories themselves, frequently misunderstand the rather simple idea of metaphor in the Fourth Gospel.[31] Here in John,

---

and John. Anderson, *The Riddles of the Fourth Gospel*, 126.

28. Martyn, *History and Theology in the Fourth Gospel*, 35–66.

29. Ibid., 35–66, 85–89. See also Ashton, *The Interpretation of John*, 12–13.

30. Soulen, *Handbook of Biblical Criticism*, 65.

31. For the list of misunderstandings in John, see Culpepper, *Anatomy of the Fourth Gospel*, 161–62. See also Stibbe, *John*, 157–58. Scriptural references include the following: 2:19–21; 3:3–5; 4:10–15, 31–34; 6:32–35, 51–53; 7:33–36; 8:21–22, 31–35; 8:51–53, 56–58; 11:11–15, 23–25; 12:32–34; 13:36–38; 14:4–6, 7–9; 16:16–19.

Jews are angry at Jesus' talk of his flesh and blood, and his disciples murmur that this is a difficult teaching.

As we see here, because the literalist reading does not capture the power of metaphors or symbols in the Fourth Gospel, extreme care should be taken so that we do not limit the diversity of symbolic or metaphoric meanings.[32] Interpretation of symbols or metaphors involves the following two steps: 1) recognizing the diversity of meaning; and 2) deciding the meaning to be taken, given the literary and historical context. Among many metaphors in the Gospel, perhaps the most important are "the Logos becoming flesh" (John 1:14) and the seven "I am" sayings of Jesus that involve metaphors such as water, bread, and the way.

However, reading the Fourth Gospel through metaphors should be linked with the historical reality of the event of Jesus and the experience of the Johannine community. Since the Fourth Gospel is a historical, theological story about Jesus and the Johannine community alike, we have to consider three aspects in tandem: history, literature, and transformation. *History* as particular times and stories of people and communities, pushes us to read and interpret Jewish history, Jesus, and the Johannine community from various perspectives so that our understanding may be enriched. The task of the historian is not simply to dig into ancient remains (archaeological excavation), but to interpret them from one's own context. Much *literature* is the written records and stories that reflect the realities of a historical people

---

32. Regarding the example of the diversity of metaphorical meaning, we may consider the following: the body as a metaphor (in Paul's letters) may mean various things—the body as a community (egalitarian or hierarchical), the body as a locus of life, the body as cosmic body, the body as an essence of the important thing, etc. If we read Paul's metaphoric statement "You are the body of Christ" (1 Cor 12:27), we can think of a diversity of metaphoric meaning because the subject "you" can be explained in many different ways. That is, the life of "you" is complex and varied. We may think of the various possibilities of the body of Christ: 1) the body as a community belonging to Christ; 2) the body as a hierarchical social body; 3) the body as an egalitarian community; 4) the body as a mystical union with Christ; 5) the body as Christ's own body (physical or metaphorical); 6) the body as Christ's broken body (the crucified body); and 7) the body as the locus of life (a metaphor for a way of life). As we see above, the options are many, but it does not mean all are valid. When we go through this list, we have to determine the best option in terms of the spirit of the letter. For more, see Kim, *Christ's Body in Corinth*, 11–38.

and through which our understanding of history may be deepened. *Transformation* can include a change of status, belief, attitude, or vision for utopia for persons and/or communities. These changes can often be detected in a group's history and literature.

Sociological readings of the Fourth Gospel too often stop at the identification of a "sectarian community" that seeks its own survival and prosperity. In this book I want to take one step further, exploring not only the historical community, but also the engaging power of the gospel for this community and the world. If God is the God of love in the Fourth Gospel, if Jesus' primary mission is to embody God's presence, the logical consequence, I want to say, is that the Johannine Christians are also to follow the way of Jesus for God and the world. Our personal relationships with God and fellow human beings can be renewed, based on God's abundant love and justice for the world. Our political lives can be transformed according to God's unbiased love of the world that needs life and light. Those who are hungry and thirsty have to be satisfied because it is God's will. Evil and darkness should be resisted and prevented because the mission of the Logos has to affect all. Read this way, the Fourth Gospel possesses a valuable source for human transformation. If we focus on Jesus' divinity without unpacking the work of Jesus as the Son of God, we will miss the central message conveyed in the Fourth Gospel, which is none other than to give life and light to the world.

CHAPTER OUTLINES

In chapter 2, we will examine the various backgrounds and contexts of the "I am" sayings in the Hebrew Bible, the Greco-Roman world, and first-century Palestinian Judaism. The main question here is how or to what degree we can relate ancient contexts to Johannine literature and the Johannine community. In chapter 3, we will examine the overall context of the Fourth Gospel with a focus on the conditions and issues of the Johannine community. In addition, we will also explore the Fourth Gospel's relation to the early Jesus tradition in order to know how the "I am" sayings of Jesus derive from his core teaching. In chapter 4, we will explore the entire narrative of the Fourth Gospel with a focus on the outlines and structure of the Logos. The focus here is to see how Jesus as the Son of God embodies the Logos of God through his life and death. In chapter 5, we will explore the process of transformation in the Johannine narrative. The focus here will be John 14:6 as a central text for that purpose. A plethora of metaphors and symbols in the Fourth Gospel will be reconstructed in view of their symbolic transformative space. In chapter 6, we will see how the Johannine community itself undergoes the process of transformation. Chapter 7 circles back to the question of the Christology raised in the Introduction. This chapter concludes with the implications of this study for today's pluralistic society.

2

"I Am" Sayings in Jewish and Hellenistic Traditions

"I am" sayings of Jesus or the Logos in the Fourth Gospel may be associated with the Hebrew noun *dabar* (spoken word) in the Old Testament, which connotes various things: God's judgment (Hos 1:1; Joel 1:1); God's law (Deut 32:46–47); God's healing power (Ps 107:20); God's light for people (Ps 119:105); God's creative power (Ps 33:6); and God's wisdom (Prov 8:27–30, 35; Wis 7:25–26; 9:1–2, 9–10; Sir 1:1).[33] On the other hand, "I am" sayings of Jesus are also related to Exod 3:14 (*ehyeh asher ehyeh*: "I am who I am" or "I shall be what I shall be"). Others look at Hellenistic culture and philosophy as a more sustainable backdrop for the Fourth Gospel.[34] Among all of these references about the Logos, Exod 3:14 (*ehyeh asher ehyeh*: "I am who I am" or "I shall be that I shall be") stands out because Jesus' "I am" sayings are often associated with the divine connection.

---

33. See Brown, *John*, 1:519–24; Ashton, *Studying John*, 5–35.

34. See Scott, *Sophia and the Johannine Jesus*, 83–173. See also Schüssler Fiorenza, *In Memory of Her*, 133–34; and Wainwright, "Jesus Sophia: An Image Obscured in the Johannine Prologue," 92–97.

REVIEW OF EXOD 3:14

There are a few options for reading Exod 3:14. First, the most popular, long-held traditional reading is called the *onto-theological reading* where *ehyeh asher ehyeh* is translated ontologically: "I am the one who exists" (*ego eimi ho on* in the Septuagint).[35] The idea here is that God exists forever, and this clause denotes either divine name revelation or divine character. Some New Testament readers relate the "I am" sayings of Jesus to this idea.

There is a second and different reading called *idem per idem* ("same for same"), a technique that rejects name calling altogether. The repetition of "I am" emphasizes the same person of *I*. God cannot be named properly in any human language.[36] While Moses is anxious about God's name, God cannot be adequately explained by name. Moreover, as Buber highlights, in some ancient cultures there was a tendency for names to be misrepresented for personal reasons:

> The true nature of a person is the essence of the person, distilled from his real being, so that he is present in it once again. What is more, he is present in it in such a form that anybody who knows the true name and knows how to pronounce it in the correct way can gain control of him. The person himself is unapproachable, he offers resistance; but through the name he becomes approachable, the speaker has power over him.[37]

Third, there is an *eschatological reading* that emphasizes God's ongoing promise and faithfulness toward his people.[38] This reading works well in terms of God's covenant with his people. In this reading, *ehyeh asher ehyeh* indicates God's promise in the future: "I will be

---

35. This translation reflects the Greek philosophy that goes back to Parmenides and Plato who associate God with *being*. See Feldman, *Judaism and Hellenism Reconsidered*, 62. See also Philo, *Life of Moses* 1.74–75; *On Dreams* 1.230–31.

36. This kind of logic can be applied to humans too. Each person is unique and therefore cannot be adequately represented by a name. Every one has a unique "I am."

37. Buber, *Moses*, 61.

38. See McCarthy, "Exodus 3:14: History, Philosophy and Theology," 311–22. See also Brevard Childs, *The Book of Exodus*, 83–88.

what I will be." Actually, the Hebrew verb *hyh* ("to be") in 3:14 is *qal*, an imperfect form that has the ongoing aspect of the to-be verb. God is sovereign now and in the future.[39]

Fourth, there is a reading of Jewish *Midrash* that emphasizes God's redemption to those in Babylonian exile.[40] When people live in exile without hope, they need a new hope of salvation in God. So the story of the burning bush in the wilderness reflects their exile situation. Symbolically speaking, however, the burning bush also stands for a beacon of light that shines upon the world. Like the burning bush that is not consumed, exiled Jews see a hope of liberation and of becoming a light to the nations.

ALTERNATIVE READING OF EHYEH ASHER EHYEH

Ehyeh asher ehyeh can be understood in the larger context of the oppression and liberation of Israelites. That is, the context of the burning bush episode and *ehyeh asher ehyeh* (3:14) have to do with God's plan to liberate his people from slavery in Egypt, as Exod 3:7-8 reads:

> Then the Lord said, "I have observed the misery of my people who are in Egypt; I have heard their cry on account of their taskmasters. Indeed, I know their sufferings, and I have come down to deliver them from the Egyptians, and to bring them up out of that land to a good and broad land, a land flowing with milk and honey, to the country of the Canaanites, the Hittites, the Amorites, the Perizzites, the Hivites, and the Jebusites."

For God's plan of liberation of the Israelites from slavery, Moses is called out and sent to the Israelites. God says to Moses, "I am the God of your ancestors." However, Moses is not confident about that calling, and he asks: "Who am I that I should go to Pharaoh, and bring the Israelites out of Egypt?" (Exod 3:11). Then God assures Moses, "I will be with you." But Moses is not content with that answer

---

39. Hazony, *The Philosophy of Hebrew Scripture*, 244. See also Fishbane, *Biblical Text and Texture*, 67–71; Levenson, *Sinai and Zion*, 22; Buber, *Moses*, 51–54.

40. Dreyfus, "The burning bush through the eyes of midrashi: God's word then and now," 62–75.

either and asks again, "If I come to the Israelites and say to them, 'The God of your ancestors has sent me to you,' and they ask me, 'What is his name?' what shall I say to them?" (3:13). Now God responds to Moses in a somewhat mysterious or unexpected way: *ehyeh asher ehyeh* (3:14), which I take to mean "I shall be what I shall be." While Moses wants God's name, God wants Moses to have confidence that God will be with him. If we rephrase what God seems to say here, it might be like this: "It's me, Moses! I am the same God who appeared to your ancestors and I will be with you; I am the God who was, is, and will be." God promises his sovereign presence of "I am" in the context of the oppression and liberation of the Israelites. In this way, *ehyeh asher ehyeh* is not a divine name or divine character; rather, it is the language of God's promise and protection for the Israelites.[41]

For God's plan of liberation for the Israelites, Moses needs a renewal of mind and heart.[42] In other words, the burning bush episode (Exod 2:21—3:16) becomes a story of his transformation that involves his identity and his view of the world. Moses encounters the mysterious site/sight of a burning bush, and turns aside to see why the bush is not being burnt up. That the bush would burn without being consumed seems like a logical fallacy beyond his understanding of the world. Moses knows for sure that a bush in the wilderness is dry or worthless, easily burned. So he is speechless about this "unreasonable" sight/site. Nothing that he knows through experience can adequately explain this. At this very moment, God calls Moses, and Moses answers, "Here I am!" Moses meets the wholly mysterious Other. But God warns: "Come no closer! Remove the sandals from your feet, for the place on which you are standing is holy ground" (3:5). Moses must begin in the wilderness, the place of hopelessness, in a similar situation to the Israelites, who are enslaved in Egypt. The holy ground is not anywhere else than right here, the burning bush in the wilderness that represents both weakness and hope. Though the Israelites are like the burning bush now, they will be given a new life and serve as a beacon of light for the world. Because of the experience

41. In fact, the divine name YHWH appears in the next verses 3:15–16. This further implies that the *ehyeh asher ehyeh* does not represent a divine name or character.

42. This section is adapted from my earlier work, Kim, *A Transformative Reading of the Bible*, 34.

with the burning bush, Moses is reborn with a renewed sense of who he is and what he has to do for the holy land where the Israelites can live. His identity is firmly rooted in the God of promise and hope. Moses is ready to go out for God and the Israelites; he is treated like a god because of his mission: "The Lord said to Moses, 'See, I have made you like God to Pharaoh'" (Exod 7:1; cf. 4:16). Moses is transformed in that he now foresees a reality of liberation for the Israelites.

In summary, the burning bush story and *ehyeh asher ehyeh* can be best understood as the story of liberation and transformation in which Moses is called out and commissioned for the Israelites. Similarly, God sends Jesus in the Fourth Gospel for the mission of liberation of the people dwelling in darkness. In this way, the "I am" sayings of Jesus are not connected to the theophany of YHWH before Moses at the burning bush; rather, they are meant to be the work of Jesus for God.[43]

"I AM" SAYINGS IN HEBREW SCRIPTURES

Besides *ehyeh asher ehyeh* in Exod 3:14, there are plenty of "I am" sayings about Yahweh in the Hebrew Bible. One typical form is the first person pronoun (*anochi* or *ani*) combined with Yahweh. For example: "I am the Lord your God, who has brought you out from the land of Egypt, from the house of bondage" (Exod 20:2; see also Deut 29:1–5; Hos 13:4). Similarly, Isaiah 43:3 reads: "For I am the Lord your God, the holy one of Israel, your savior." The other form, *ani hu* ("I am he") is also found in several places (for example: Isa 41:4; 43:10, 13, 25; 44:6; 46:4; 48:12; 51:12; 52:6; Deut 32:39; Ps 102:28).

In both forms, God is portrayed as both the deliverer of his people and the sovereign liberator.[44] God cares for the poor, orphans, widows, and foreigners. When there is no justice in society, God speaks to his agents or prophets who deliver God's word to the people. "Thus says the Lord" (Isa 22:17–20; Jer 9:1–2) is a prophetic formula

---

43. Williams, "I am He," 16–54. Paul Anderson adds his affirmation to Williams's reading: "The significance of Williams' contribution is that it clarifies the prevalent I-am claims of Yahweh in scripture, connecting the saving action of Yahweh—rather than his divine being—with Jesus' I-am sayings in John" (Anderson, "The Origin and Development of the Johannine *Ego Eimi*," 16).

44. See Williams, "I am He," 16–54; Ball, *"I Am" in John's Gospel*.

found in the prophets from Isaiah to Amos. For example: "For thus says the Lord to the house of Israel: Seek me and live; but do not seek Bethel, and do not enter into Gilgal or cross over to Beer-sheba; for Gilgal shall surely go into exile, and Bethel shall come to nothing" (Amos 5:4–6). Amos speaks for God and acts out the divine speech of "I am" for the people. The purpose of the divine speech is to urge them to turn to God (the Hebrew verb *shub*, meaning a change of heart and a return to God).[45] Furthermore, the divine "I am" sayings are expressed through the personified wisdom in a female figure.[46] For example, Prov 1:1 and 23 read: "Wisdom cries aloud in the plaza; she gives her voice in the square . . . Turn at my warning; behold, I will pour out my spirit to you; I will make my words known to you." Similarly, Sir 24:18 and 24 read: "I am the mother of beautiful love, of fear, of knowledge, and of holy hope; being eternal, I am given to all my children, to those who are named by the one . . . Do not cease to be strong in Yahweh . . . Yahweh-Shadhay alone is the God, and besides other one there is no savior."

In sum, the "I am" sayings in the Hebrew Bible can be understood as God's character and his work of liberation, justice, and peace. At the same time, those sayings are close to the work of the Spirit. By analogy, as we will see in the next chapters, Jesus in the Fourth Gospel can be understood as the Son of God who carries out the work of God.

"I AM" SAYINGS IN THE GRECO-ROMAN WORLD

There are two kinds of "I am" sayings in the Greco-Roman world: that of the emperor (Caesar) and that of the mystery religions. Caesar is claimed as the Son of God (*divi filius*) and retains the most honorable

---

45. Prophets urge people to turn to God, not to people or any other thing. *Shub* in the Hebrew Bible generally means "to turn back" from evil and "to turn to God." See for example: Isa 9:13; Zech 1:4; Jer 31:19; Hos 3:1; 7:16. In this context, the meaning of *shub* is close to that expressed in Amos: "Seek the Lord and live" (Amos 5:4–6).

46. Regarding the study of wisdom mythology, see Schüssler Fiorenza, "Wisdom Mythology and the Christological Hymns of the New Testament," 17–41. For the relation of Sophia with John's Jesus, see Scott, *Sophia and the Johannine Jesus*, 80. See also Schroer, "The Book of Sophia," 17–38.

titles: Augustus (the revered one), Imperator (commander-in-chief), Imperium Maius (absolute power), Pontifex Maximus (chief priest), and Princeps (First Citizen). Augustus boasts of his major achievements in the first person of "I did this or that" in the inscription *Res Gestae Divi Augusti* (The Deeds of the Divine Augustus). But his achievements are results of military campaigns and tactics. The lower classes of people do not participate in these achievements. It is in this context that ordinary people will search for something to express their hopes for a better future, and indeed, many folk religions or mystery religions developed and flourished in this time.[47] For example, Isis, a goddess of fertility, listens to prayers of the people and provides them with comfort, hopes, and encouragement. Here we can consider the "I am" sayings of Isis:

> I am Isis, the lord of every land. . . .
> I gave and ordained laws for men, which no one is able to change.
> I am eldest daughter of Kronos. I am wife and sister of King Osiris. . . .
> I divided the earth from the heaven. I showed the paths of the stars. . . .
> I brought together woman and man. . . .
> I broke down the governments of tyrants. . . .
> I established penalties for those who practice injustice.
> I decreed mercy to suppliants. With me the right prevails. . . .
> I set free these in bonds.[48]

Here Isis takes the role similar to that of Yahweh and provides assurance that people will find hope through her. The "I am" sayings of Isis typify the need for a perfect world where humanity lives with justice. Similarly, we find the "I am" sayings in "Thunder, Perfect Mind" of the Nag Hammadi library: "I am the first and the last. I am she who is honored and she who is disgrace. I am the harlot and the holy one

47. Smith, "Prolegomena to a Discussion of Aretalogies," 174–99. See also Kee, "Aretalogy and Gospel," 402–22.

48. Kraemer, *Maenads, Martyrs, Matrons, Monastics,* 368–70. See also Arthur, *The Wisdom Goddess: Feminist Motifs in Eight Nag Hammadi Documents,* 161–62; Trombley, "Prolegomena to the Systemic Analysis of Late Hellenistic Religion," 95–113.

. . . I am unlearned, and they learn from me . . . I am a mute unable to speak, and great is the quantity of my words."[49] Here we see a kind of subversive wisdom that challenges a patriarchal view.[50] The role of the "I am" sayings of Isis is not meant for establishing divine identity but for supporting people in chaos, confusion, and bondage due to social unrest. Isis is another name of a liberator. The religion is not separate from every day life.

SUMMARY

In this chapter, we have explored the immediate context of Exod 3:14 (*ehyeh asher ehyeh*) and the burning bush episode, which has to do with God's plan of liberation of the Israelites. Though Hellenistic Judaism understands *ehyeh asher ehyeh* (Exod 3:14) as the divine essence or character ("I am the one who exists"), its literary context has more to do with God's steadfast love and commitment to his people in bondage. We also have explored a wide array of contexts of the "I am" sayings in the Hebrew Bible, Jewish traditions, and the Greco-Roman world. In the Hebrew Bible God speaks through his prophets with the form of "Thus says the Lord" when there is no justice. Wisdom also shouts on the street because God's presence requires justice in the world. In the Greco-Roman world, Caesar speaks about his own accomplishments at the expense of the lower class and foreign vassals. This is the context where folk religions flourish and fill in the gap of emptiness and insecurity. Similarly, the "I am" sayings of Jesus in the Fourth Gospel can be understood as providing a symbolic transformative space for those who are struggling in the world.

---

49. Arthur, *Wisdom Goddess*, 218–25
50. McGuire, "Thunder, Perfect Mind," 39–54.

3

The Historical and Literary Context of the Fourth Gospel

The Fourth Gospel is very different from the Synoptic Gospels in terms of source material, style of writing, and theological orientation. These differences might explain why scholars prefer the Synoptic Gospels to the Fourth Gospel for the study of the historical Jesus.[51] The Fourth Gospel is dubbed as a maverick gospel distant from the message of the historical Jesus. But this view is largely inaccurate. For example, though there are no extensive teachings about the important theme of the kingdom of God in the Fourth Gospel, there are important mentions of "the kingdom of God" (3:3, 5; 18:36).

51. The so-called Jesus Seminar did not consider any sayings of Jesus in the Fourth Gospel as authentic. See Funk and Hoover, *The Five Gospels: The Search for the Authentic Words of Jesus*, 11–20. See also Crossan, *the Historical Jesus*. Ernst Käsemann says, "It can hardly be doubted that the Synoptists intended in all good faith to give their readers authentic tradition about Jesus. But it is impossible to ascribe the same intention to the fourth Evangelist . . . It is now widely acknowledged that for him the merely historical only has interest and value to the extent to which it mirrors symbolically the recurring experiences of Christian faith" (Käsemann, *Essays on New Testament Themes*, 22). Similarly, Günther Bornkamm says, "The Gospel according to John has so different a character in comparison with the other three, and is to such a degree the product of a developed theological reflection, that we can only treat it as a secondary source" (Bornkamm, *Jesus of Nazareth*, 14).

In John 3:3, Jesus emphasizes that one must be "born from above to see the kingdom of God." That is, all human thoughts and actions should begin with God, the source of life. The Logos is another name of God's life, power, or Spirit. In this sense, spiritual birth in John 3 must be the language of Jesus, as Marcus Borg understands the historical Jesus to be deeply spiritual and interested in a change of society and culture.[52] If we understand this way, Jesus' teaching about the kingdom of God in John 3:3, 5 is very inclusive of every aspect of human life: personal, political, and ethical. Moreover, in John 18:36, Jesus again talks about the kingdom of God when he is at trial before Pilate: "My kingdom is not from this world." Understanding this as a kind of apolitical statement is not correct. Rather, Jesus challenges Pilate's kingdom and says his message and work of the kingdom of God is not based on worldly powers, but in God or the Spirit. Is not this kind of response close to the historical Jesus?[53]

While there are clear differences among all four Gospels, we can hardly say that the Fourth Gospel is less historical than the Synoptic Gospels. Whereas in the Synoptic Gospels Jesus' main topic is the kingdom of God and uses parables to communicate, in the Fourth Gospel he uses metaphors and symbols (wind, water, bread, light,

---

52. Borg, *Jesus: A New Vision*, 141–50. According to Borg, Jesus was a Spirit-filled person who sought to change the religious social world of first-century Palestine. Borg works on the two organizing principles: Spirit and culture. Borg claims that the world of the Spirit is real and Jesus had deep, intimate relationships with the Spirit. The author does not stop here but relates this reality of the Spirit with culture. That is to say, a Spirit-filled person could not remove himself from the culture in which he lived. In discussing the world of the Spirit, Borg states that the reality of the Spirit has been present not only in the biblical tradition but also in the social-scientific studies of paranormal experiences (universal primordial tradition). In the biblical tradition, Israel's story itself was the story of the interaction between the world of the Spirit and the world of ordinary experiences. The Spirit of the world became part of their lives. Moses and the prophets were also Spirit-filled mediators. In social-scientific studies of paranormal experiences, cross-culturally, the world of Spirit has also been accessed by the charismatic who entered it and experienced the world of the Spirit.

53. Because of the discovery of the Dead Sea Scrolls, we now learn that the Fourth Gospel should be studied "in terms of first-century Palestinian Jewish writings, especially the Dead Sea Scrolls." See Charlesworth, "The Dead Scrolls and the Gospel according to John," 65–97. As such, the Fourth Gospel conveys facts and experiences of the early Christian movement in the late first century.

way, etc.) to communicate the Logos of God. Though the Fourth Gospel is different from the Synoptic Gospels, in some cases it shares material with them. For example, it includes "geographical and narrative details, many of the events of Jesus' ministry, and quite a few sayings, including some material most typical of John."[54]

In fact, the Fourth Gospel may contain more of the historical Jesus source.[55] For example, there is information about Jewish customs and locales (2:6, 13; 5:1; 6:4; 7:2; 11:55; 19:40, 42); low christological terms expressed through Jewish or Aramaic language (1:38, 49; 3:2; 4:31; 6:25; 9:2; 11:8; 20:16); and conflict with Jews in the synagogue (7:13; 9:22; 19:38). We also see various Jewish festivals such as the Dedication. Whereas the Synoptic Gospels portray Passover as a pivotal event in Jesus' ministry, making it a more dramatic event, the Fourth Gospel mentions Passover three times, which is more realistic in the sense that Jesus goes up to Jerusalem and comes back and forth several times. Although the language and style of the Fourth Gospel significantly differs from the Synoptic Gospels, the essence of the message seems close to the historical Jesus who embodies the love of God in the world. For example, the Fourth Gospel puts the episode of Jesus' cleansing of the Temple early in the narrative, in chapter 2, to emphasize Jesus' prophetic ministry that renews the Temple (John 2:13–22). In a way, Jesus is compared to Jeremiah who speaks about the renewal of the heart at the brink of a national disaster. The centerpiece of Jeremiah's prophecy is that the Lord will make a new covenant with the house of Israel and the house of Judah, not because the old covenant is wrong but because the Israelites

54. Thompson, "The Historical Jesus and the Johannine Christ," 21–42. Thompson lists a few sayings found both in John and Synoptics: John 3:8 with Mark 4:27; John 3:35 and 5:19–20a with Matt 11:27; John 5:23 with Matt 10:40; John 12:47 with Luke 9:56; John 13:13–16 with Matt 10:24–25; John 16:2 with Matt 24:9. See also Dunn, "John and the Oral Gospel Tradition," 351–79. See Anderson, *The Riddles of the Fourth Gospel*, 126–28. Anderson argues that Mark and John are two separate gospel traditions based on early Christian experience.

55. Most recently, the John, Jesus, and History Group of the Society of Biblical Literature made significant contributions to our understanding of the historicity of this Gospel in connection with the historical Jesus. I think this is a right movement since this Fourth Gospel has been misrepresented as if it were an anomaly from the perspective of the historical Jesus or from the view of the Synoptic Gospels. See Anderson, *The Riddles of the Fourth Gospel*, 195–219.

broke it (Jer 31:31–34). The new covenant is a matter of the heart and the Lord writes his law on their hearts. Likewise, Jesus in the Fourth Gospel asks for a renewal of the heart by seeking the source of life in God (spiritual birth in 3:1–21, for example). With this inherited prophetic tradition of Jesus, Jesus in the Fourth Gospel embodies God's love and pours out his love for the world.

THE FOURTH GOSPEL AND THE JOHANNINE COMMUNITY

As Paul Anderson argues, composition of the Fourth Gospel and the Johannine Epistles took a long period of time (80–100 CE).[56] Anderson's theory is called the two-edition theory of composition: a first edition of the Johannine Gospel (80–85 CE) and a second edition after the death of the Beloved Disciple (100 CE).[57] According to Anderson, the writing of the Johannine Epistles is placed in between these times (85–95 CE).[58] This Johannine community is founded with the testimony of the Beloved Disciple whose identity is never known, yet persists in the Gospel (13:23–25; 19:26–26; 20:1–10; 21:1–25).[59] This suggests that he continues and embodies Jesus' earthly ministry. The primary location of this community is debatable, but one of the strong candidates is Ephesus.[60] The majority of members are believed to be Jews who accept Jesus as the Jewish Messiah.

In talking about the community behind this gospel, J. Louis Martyn's thesis of a "two-level drama" is most convincing.[61]

56. Anderson, *The Riddles of the Fourth Gospel*, 141–44. On the other hand, D. Moody Smith posits the date of 90–110. See Smith, *John*, 42–43.

57. Anderson, *The Riddles of the Fourth Gospel*, 141–42.

58. Ibid., 142.

59. The Fourth Gospel balances the role of the beloved disciple with that of Peter, as we see in chapter 21 where the risen Lord recognizes the important roles of Peter and the beloved disciple. Peter goes on with the death of a martyr while the beloved disciple has a job to transmit the Jesus tradition to later people. This fact suggests that the Johannine community embraces and reconciles with the Jewish Christianity (represented by Peter), and extends the radical love of God for all.

60. Smith, *John*, 39–41.

61. Martyn, *History and Theology*, 35–66. According to him, those who

According to Martyn, the Fourth Gospel can be read as a story of Jesus, and at the same time it can be read as a story of the Johannine community in conflict with mainline Judaism.[62] On the one hand, the Fourth Gospel tradition goes back to Jesus in his historical ministry where he has conflict with Jews because of his teaching and preaching about the kingdom of God. Jesus emphasizes the transformation of the world and is yet opposed and persecuted because of his work for God. On the other hand, this Gospel contains the very story of struggle in the Johannine community members in conflict with the Jewish synagogue around 85–90 CE, as we get clues about their separation from the synagogue because of their confession of Jesus as the Messiah (John 7:13; 9:22; 19:38).

The other context of the Johannine community is an imperial one. There are several parts of the Johannine literature that implicitly challenge the rule of the Empire, as Warren Carter notes in reading the Fourth Gospel through the perspective of the community's survival and maintenance of their faith.[63] In my view, his political approach to the early Christian community and the Fourth Gospel is correct, something that we often have missed out in our study of the Christian material. While an imperial reading is important, our reading should expand to include religious conflict and internal matters of the community.

---

confess that Jesus is the Christ were persecuted and expelled from the synagogue, and the Fourth Gospel reflects a story of struggle and a story of faith at the same time. Though the historical evidence of expulsion is debatable because Jewish Benedictions may not be a decisive clue as some argue against Martyn, I think what really matters is not the historical evidence that this community was expelled but the existence of this kind of conflict with a possible community we call Johannine. Historically speaking, this kind of conflict may have been persistent in the work of the historical Jesus if he preached about the radical kingdom of God in a manner that Jewish leaders did not like.

62. Regarding the Jewish background of the Fourth Gospel, see Davies, "Reflections on Aspects of the Jewish Background of the Gospel of John," 43–64.

63. See Carter, *John and Empire: Initial Explorations.* See also Scott, *Domination and the Arts of Resistance: Hidden Transcripts,* 5–28.

SUMMARY

In this chapter, we have explored various contexts of the Fourth Gospel and its literary relation to the other gospels including Jesus tradition. We also looked at the matters of community conflict in the synagogue and outside of it. Christ-followers' (Christian-Jews') confession that Christ crucified is the Son of God and the Messiah is indeed a dangerous political claim because Caesar is the only son of God in the Empire. More than that, the Johannine community members are isolated and expelled from the synagogue because of their faith in Jesus as the Jewish Messiah. The Johannine community needs comfort and encouragement and transformation in order to maintain their faith. Given the nature of their difficult community life because of this new faith, one of the most important issues it faces is how to survive and grow in its present situation. Moreover, the issue concerns how they may overcome the difficulties caused by a separation of the community and life in the harsh Roman environment. How is the community transformed?

4

"I Am" Sayings
in the Fourth Gospel

In this chapter, we will explore the "I am" sayings of Jesus in the Fourth Gospel with a focus on the theme of the Logos, which represents the power and presence of God. Jesus as the Son of God incarnates the Logos and does the work of God. Accordingly, "I am" sayings of Jesus are understood as his expression and action for the Logos of God, which is interchangeable with the Spirit of God.[64] To explore this theme, we will ask the following: How is the Logos introduced and incarnated with Jesus? What is the meaning of the Logos becoming flesh? How does Jesus journey with it? What are the content and the cost of the embodiment of the Logos?

OUTLINE OF LOGOS JOURNEY

"Logos journey" is a metaphor that explains the origin, departure, work, and return of the Logos as the Spirit, power, or wisdom of God.[65] In this sense, the Logos is the subject of the Fourth Gospel,

64. See note 5 in chapter 1.

65. For an analysis of the Logos journey, the Fourth Gospel as a whole, including chap. 21, will be examined. Chapter 21 is an integral part of the whole Gospel, not merely an addition to the Gospel. For this argument, see Culpepper,

appearing in 1:1 and throughout the text. The idea of Logos journey would not seem strange to the ears of the Johannine community or first-century Jewish readers because they were familiar with this notion of the Spirit of God. When God created heaven and earth, the Spirit of God swept over the face of the waters (Gen 1:2), and this Spirit is working through all godly activities, through God's prophets and other agents. It is the source of wisdom and personification of God-being-in-the-world.

This Logos of God became flesh (1:14)—a theology of radical incarnation that is manifest through Jesus' life and death. While Jesus is not the Logos per se, he lives with and for the Logos, journeying with it until the end of his life. As Jesus finishes his journey with the Logos, the Logos re-incarnates with Jesus' disciples and his followers. When Jesus leaves, the Advocate (*parakletos*) comes to the world and continues the work of Jesus. In this way, the Logos journey comes full circle. With this idea of the Logos journey, we may outline the entire Gospel.

Outline of the Fourth Gospel

I. The Logos introduced (1:1–18):

    A. Origin of the Logos (1:1–5)

    B. Testimony of the Logos (1:6–13)

    C. The Logos incarnate (1:14–18)

II. Jesus' journey with the Logos (1:19—17:26):

    A. Testimony of John the Baptist (1:19–34)

    B. The gathering of the first disciples (1:35–51)

    C. The work of the Logos (2:1—5:47)

        1. The wedding at Cana (2:1–12)

        2. Jesus in Jerusalem (2:13—3:21)

            a. The cleansing of the Temple (2:13–22)

            b. Jesus and Nicodemus (2:23—3:21)

"Designs for the Church in the Imagery of John 21:1–14."

B. The risen Lord with Peter: "feed my sheep" (21:15-19)

C. The risen Lord with the Beloved Disciple (21:20-25)

EXCURSUS: OVERVIEW OF THE "I AM" SAYINGS IN THE FOURTH GOSPEL

The "I am" sayings of other people

There are three types of "I am" sayings in the Fourth Gospel. The first type is found in persons other than Jesus. For example, the blind man insists that he is the same person who was blind and now sees. He says, "I am [*ego eimi*]" (9:9). Peter denies that he is not one of Jesus' disciples at the scene of Jesus' trial and he says, "I am not" (18:17, 25).

The "I am" sayings of Jesus without the predicate

Among the "I am" sayings of Jesus, there are two kinds: the absolute sayings of "I am" without a predicate and the sayings of "I am" with the predicate. The most typical form of an absolute saying is found in "I am" only ("it is I"). For example, Jesus answers with "I am" when disciples are terrified at Jesus' walking on the water (6:20). This saying may not differ from the blind man's affirmation of his identity. Jesus simply affirms his identity: "It's me." References regarding this absolute form are found also in the following: 4:26; 8:24; 8:28; 8:58; 12:26; 13:13; and 13:19. Most of these references are used in referring to Jesus' identity. For example, when Jesus says in 8:58, "*I am* before Abraham was," it does not mean something literally to support the idea of his preexistence or divinity. The context has to do with the Johannine community's belief that Jesus is the Jewish Messiah, and such hyperbolic language challenges those Jews who claim a unique position or privilege ("We are Moses' disciples"). The point of Jesus' saying here is not so much about his identity, but rather it is about God's sovereignty by which all are included in the love of God.

The "I am" saying of Jesus with the predicate

The other forms of the "I am" sayings come with predicates. In the Fourth Gospel there are seven "I am" sayings of Jesus that include the predicate nominative: "I am the bread of life / living bread (6:35–51); "I am the light of the world" (8:12; see also 9:5); "I am the gate of the sheepfold" (10:7–9); "I am the good shepherd" (10:11–14); "I am the resurrection and the life" (11:25); "I am the way, the truth, and the life" (14:6); "I am the vine / true vine" (15:1–5).[66] Taking an example of John 14:6a, the structure of this saying is as follows: *Ego* (first-person pronoun, nominative) *eimi* (first-person, "to be" verb) *he hodos* (feminine noun, singular, nominative). That is, "I am the way." Here "the way" is a predicate. We have other predicates: the bread of life, the light of the world, the gate, the shepherd, the resurrection, the way-truth-life, and vine. If these are considered metaphors, what is the intended meaning of these sayings?

For example, what is the meaning of "I am the light"? How is Jesus understood in terms of the light? We can consider several options: 1) Jesus' origin is the light (he is the

---

66. For a comparison of the "I am" sayings with the Synoptic Gospels, see Anderson, "The Origin and Development of the Johannine *Ego Eimi* Sayings in Cognitive-Critical Perspective." In this article, Anderson argues that the themes and forms of the "I am" sayings in the Fourth Gospel are also found in the Synoptic Gospels. In so doing, his point is that the Johannine "I am" sayings are distinct but not unique. According to Anderson, the Fourth Gospel and Mark are considered two different, independent traditions ("Bi-Optic Gospels"); both are based on historical memories of Jesus event. For a more detailed research about the "I am" sayings, see Ball, *"I Am" in John's Gospel*; Brown, *The Gospel According to John (i–xii)*, 533–38; Comfort, *I Am the Way: A Spiritual Through the Gospel of John*; Harner, *The "I Am" of the Fourth Gospel: A Study in Johannine Usage and Thought*; Neyrey, "'I Am the Door' (John 10.7, 9): Jesus the Broker in the Fourth Gospel," 271–91; Schnackenburg, "The Origin and Meaning of the *ego eimi* Formula," 79–89; Schweizer, *Ego Eimi*; Stauffer, *Jesus and his Story*, 174–95; Williams, *"I am He": The Meaning and Interpretation of "ANI HU"*; Williams, "'I Am' or 'I Am He'?," 343–52.

light); 2) Jesus brings the light (revealer of the light); 3) Jesus testifies to the light by doing the work of God (Jesus' work is the light). Option 1 may work if that is understood in the setting of confession at worship. Otherwise, it may not work well because in the Fourth Gospel the light appears before Jesus. The Logos and the light come together. The subject of the prologue until John 1:13 is the light, not Jesus, although the connection with Jesus is insinuated. But a clear clue that Jesus incarnates the Logos comes at John 1:14 (the Logos becoming flesh). Strictly speaking, the Logos and the light are primordial and Jesus as God's Son incarnates these in his life and death. Through the rest of the Fourth Gospel right after the prologue, Jesus testifies to the truth and the light. It is the light that has to be trusted and lived out: "Believe in the light" (12:36). Therefore, option 1 is not acceptable.

Option 2 is different. Jesus is the revealer of the light. His identity and work help people to believe in the light (and God). Two things are emphasized: Jesus' identity and work. In other words, the point here is that only Jesus can bring the light and testify to God's truth, way, and life. Option 3 is similar to Option 2. In this option, Jesus' work is the light. What he does as God's Son produces the light for the people. Analyzing the Fourth Gospel as a whole, options 2 and 3 are workable. But in my view, option 3 may be the best, because of Jesus' sayings in the Fourth Gospel. Jesus always emphasizes his working relationship with the Father (4:34; 10:25–30). Jesus asks people to believe his work for God and to believe his identity from God. In an ultimate case, if there is no work for God, the equation between "I and the light" collapses. The same is true for the other metaphors. The primary logic of these sayings is that Jesus incarnates the Logos in various ways or with various symbols.

On the basis of the above outline of the Logos journey, we will explore how the Logos is introduced, worked out, opposed, and yet re-incarnates with Jesus' disciples after his departure.

Truth, Testimony, and Transformation

THE LOGOS INTRODUCED (1:1–18)

For the readers of the Gospel, the Logos is understood as God's wisdom or word in the Hebrew Bible, or as reason or spirit in Hellenistic philosophy. Certainly, the phrase *en arches* ("in the beginning") in John 1:1 is reminiscent of the phrase *bereshit* ("in the beginning") in Gen 1:1. If Genesis is thought to be a main idea for this verse, the Logos has to do with God's creative activity and redemption of the world (Isa 8:11; 30:20–21; 35:8). As we see in John 1:6–13, the Logos has been before Jesus,[67] available throughout Jewish and world history;[68] but the Logos was not accepted in the world because people do not want their evil acts to be exposed to the light (3:20; 7:7; 12:19–20).

The task of the Logos is to restore the world full of evil and darkness to the world full of the abundant life and light. If we understand this way, the Logos is hardly distinguishable from God or the Spirit of God. In first-century Palestine and elsewhere, Jews believed that God was present in the world through his Spirit or Logos. The Johannine Christians seem to share the same view that God's Spirit is present in the world. The Johannine community sees in Jesus' life the powerful presence of God because of his faithful, selfless, sacrificial service to God and the world. Therefore, the idea of the Logos becoming flesh should be understood in terms of the Johannine community's particular experience of God exemplified through Jesus.[69] In first-century Judaism, the Son of God is not necessarily a divine title. As Jesus the Son of God embodies the Logos of God, the Johannine community needs to follow Jesus in embodying the Logos of God.

---

67. In 1:10–13 the Greek pronoun *ho* does not refer to Jesus but to the Logos.

68. Culpepper, "Cognition in John: The Johannine Signs as Recognition Scenes," 251–60.

69. The Johannine community's particular experience can be understood with an analogy. If my daughter writes "You are the best dad in the world" on a beautiful birthday card, it does not mean I am the best dad in the world. But the point of truth claimed by my daughter is experiential or confessional. For my daughter, I am seen as the best. That is the truth, which is not a competitive or comparative truth but an experiential truth.

Purpose of the Logos

The purpose of the Logos may be found in 1:12, which is "the pivot of John's Prologue," according to Alan Culpepper.[70] In fact, 1:12 is the center of a chiastic structure in John 1:1–18 (see below): "Those who accepted the Logos receive power to become children of God."[71]

Chiasm in John 1:1–18[72]

A The Word as God and with God (1–2)
. B Creation came through the Word (3)
. . C We have received life through the Word (4–5)
. . . D John the Baptist is sent to testify (6–8)
. . . . E Incarnation and the response of the world (9–10)
. . . . . F The Word and his own (Israel) (11)
. . . . . . G Those who accepted the Word (12a)
. . . . H Authority to become children of God (12b)
. . . . . . G' Those who believed the Word (12c)
. . . . . F' The Word and his own (believers) (13)
. . . . E' Incarnation and the response of the community (14)
. . . D' The testimony of John the Baptist (15)
. . C' We have received grace through the Word (16)
. B' Grace and truth came through the Word (17)
A' The Word as God and with God (18)

"Power to become children of God" is a central idea in this text that is made possible by accepting the Logos and living with it. The Logos of God was in the world (vv. 9–10), but the world did not accept it. In the midst of this chaotic world, we find a radical shift of the textual flow in 1:14: "The Logos became flesh and lived among us, and we have seen his glory, the glory as of a father's only son, full of grace and truth." That is, God can be known and experienced

---

70. Culpepper's suggestion about the pivot of the prologue rings true when we consider the purpose of writing the Fourth Gospel as written in John 20:31: "But these are written so that you may come to believe that Jesus is the Messiah, the Son of God, and that through believing you may have eternal life in his name." See Culpepper, "The Pivot of John's Prologue," 1–31.

71. Ibid.

72. Ibid.

through the form of human life—flesh (*sarx*)—as a locus of divine revelation.

Although *sarx* (*basar* in Hebrew) is used variously in the Septuagint or in the New Testament,[73] the meaning of flesh (*sarx*) in the Fourth Gospel is positive in most cases: "the word became flesh" (1:14); "the bread is my flesh" (6:51); "my flesh and blood are life" (6:53); "my flesh and blood have eternal life" (6:54); "my flesh is true food, my blood is true drink" (6:55); and "eat my flesh and drink my blood, abide in me" (6:56). A few examples of negative use are found in the following: "the will of the flesh" (1:13); "born of flesh is flesh" (3:6); "the flesh is useless" (6:63). As we see above, flesh generally means human life as well as human life conditioned with the weak human nature, reminiscent of the dust-made human (Adam from *aphar* of the ground; Gen 2:7)—a symbol of worthlessness (Job 22:24), self-abasement (Gen 18:27; Job 42:6; Lam 3:29), and humiliation (Isa 47:1; Job 16:15; 40: 13; Ps 7:6; 44:26; 119:25).[74]

In fact, flesh is similar to life (*zoē*),[75] which occurs 47 times in the Fourth Gospel.[76] Life without flesh is unthinkable. Indeed, Jesus says he gives his life for others because he cannot ignore abuses or tortures of the flesh. Jesus shows God's love, risking his life and voluntarily giving his life for others. This is a paradox. How can Jesus give up his life since it is so precious? The answer: "Those who love their life lose it, and those who hate their life in this world will keep it for eternal life" (12:25). "No one has greater love than this, to lay down one's life for one's friends" (15:13). Furthermore, puzzling his disciples, Jesus asks them to eat his flesh and drink his blood.

In sum, the idea of incarnation in 1:14 should include several things. First, it involves a real human life (flesh) that requires a life of redemption from the evil world in which life is diminished

73. *A Greek-English Lexicon of the New Testament and Other Early Christian Literature*, 743–44.

74. *The Brown-Driver-Briggs Hebrew and English Lexicon*, 779–80.

75. Flesh connotes a person and/or life in Jewish literature and also in Hellenistic writings.

76. John 1:4 (2); 3:15–16, 36 (2); 4:14, 36; 5:21 (2), 24 (2), 26 (2), 29, 39; 6:27, 33, 35, 40, 47, 51, 53, 63 (2), 68; 8:12; 10:10–11, 15, 17, 28; 11:25; 12:25 (3), 50; 13:37–38; 14:6; 15:13; 17:2–3; 20:31.

or destroyed.[77] Second, this particular world is the place where the Logos should be discerned, testified to, and lived by people. Such is more so the case in light of an imperfect, violent world ruled by Roman domination where human life is diminished or tortured.[78] Third, the Logos becoming flesh points to Jesus who reveals who the Father is and what he wants. Jesus' understanding of his mission from God is to share the life and light with the world where there is no true light or where people block the Logos. For this mission Jesus lays down his life for the sheep (10:11, 15).

But the irony is that people do not welcome the Logos and Jesus' work of God because their evil acts can be exposed (3:20; 7:7; 12:19–20). This means following the Logos involves a cost. Some accept it and others do not. The remaining chapters contain stories about the Logos. Because Jesus incarnates the Logos, he is opposed, arrested, and put to death. There is a cost to the journey with the Logos; there is also a time of glory.

JESUS' JOURNEY WITH THE LOGOS (1:19—12:50)

After the prologue we see how Jesus incarnates the Logos and how John the Baptist and his disciples witness to it. John 3–12 reveals the works of the Logos as Jesus journeys with the Logos. Among others, we will see how Jesus interacts with Nicodemus, a Samaritan woman, a man born blind, and his disciples in the story of feeding the five thousand.

77. Rensberger, "Sectarianism and Theological Interpretation in John," 139–56. Rensberger argues that incarnational theology (1:14) must be understood radically: "God has acted in an unexpected manner, subverting religious and social establishments" (152). Moreover, he states that the idea of the Logos becoming flesh is radical to the minds of elites and philosophers in Greco-Roman times because the Logos is pure reason and the principle of the universe, which cannot be mixed or work with the flesh, which is considered perishable, inferior, belonging to the lower classes.

78. Glancy, "Torture: Flesh, Truth, and the Fourth Gospel," 107–36. Glancy emphasizes the flesh as a place of truth as she asks, "Is it possible to embrace flesh as a locus of truth and still to condemn the practice of torture?" She goes on to say: "Flesh is a truthful witness."

The Logos as the Spiritual Wind (3:1–15)

A spiritual person is born from above (*anothen* in Greek), not like a physical birth—in the sense of "again," as Nicodemus understands. Jesus talks about a different kind of birth, a new life born from "above," which connotes the Spirit or God. The spiritually born person continues to be born again and again. Such a person is like the wind, which blows freely anywhere. More importantly, as the wind is invisible and is known only by its power, the person of the Spirit is the same. A spiritual person is one who acts according to the Spirit. Where one comes from (one's identity) is not important or is simply unknown.

In this Nicodemus episode we learn that the works of the Logos have to do with a spiritual birth. A new life comes from God, the essence of the Logos, not by any human tradition or physical birth. The source of spiritual birth is God.

The Logos as the Living Water (4:4–42)

The nameless Samaritan woman in this episode is socially disenfranchised, culturally discriminated, religiously deprived, and is contrasted with Nicodemus in some respects.[79] She is tired because of her daily life as a woman and spiritually thirsty for living water.[80] On a hot day in the wilderness Jesus is tired from his journey. He meets this woman and asks for a drink of water. Jesus crosses a cultural boundary and talks to her. Through the stages of conversations between them, gradually she becomes enlightened and confesses that Jesus is the messiah who gives spiritual water.[81] In the socio-religious

79. The text does not suggest that this woman is morally ill because she has had five husbands (4:18). It is possible that she "had to marry repeatedly for economic and social reasons." See Schottroff, "The Samaritan Woman and the Notion of Sexuality in the Fourth Gospel," 157–81.

80. The temporal, geographical information sets the scene in the desert. Jesus is tired from a long journey and ends up here at Jacob's well in Samaria at noon time. Samaria is an oft-avoided passing zone to Galilee, but, as we soon see, nothing is accidental in the narrative. Readers know that Jesus' stopping at Jacob's well has a purpose when suddenly a Samaritan woman emerges to draw water while all the disciples are away to buy food.

81. Hylen, *Imperfect Believers*, 41.

context of discrimination, the metaphor of spiritual water can be understood as collapsing the hostile barriers between Jews and Gentile in that water symbolizes abundant life and equality for all. Water flows to the lower places and makes life enriched as the episode at the wedding at Cana reminds us (2:1–12). The image of water also has to do with cleansing of the temple in which now all people truly worship God through the new Messiah.[82] In the following, we will focus on conversations between Jesus and the Samaritan woman and between Jesus and the people of the city. We want to explore how the mission of the Logos is understood in these conversations.[83]

The Logos is understood in terms of living water that connotes abundant life for all. This abundance includes personal, communal, and global aspects of life: as seen in the expansion from the Samaritan woman, to her village, and to the world. Jesus helps her and her village people to worship the true God, beyond social-cultural, geographical boundaries.

Personal Water (4:7–15)

"Personal water" is a metaphor that represents the source of life in God.[84] The reader's suspense becomes higher because the scene develops between Jesus and the woman only. When Jesus asks for a drink of water, this woman, conscious of who she is as a marginalized woman, a Samaritan, bravely engages with Jesus: "How is it that you, a Jew, ask a drink of me, a woman of Samaria?" (v. 9). She is firmly

---

82. In Jewish apocalyptic literature water becomes "a symbol for eschatological cleansing": "On that day living waters shall flow out from Jerusalem" (Zech 14:8), and "water will flow from the temple" (Ezek 47:1–12). See Culpepper, *John*, 140. Similarly, we find the "living water" in the Qumran Scrolls: CD 3:16–17; 6:2–6; 19:34; 1QH 15:4, 6–7a, 13b–14a, 16). In these writings, the well (water) represents the study of scripture (Torah), which sustains the life of community. In the Fourth Gospel, however, Jesus as the living water should not be understood as replacing the Torah or Judaism; but through his life and work, God's word is manifest abundantly.

83. Hylen, *Imperfect Believers*, 43–55.

84. In the conversation of Jesus and the Samaritan woman, the water theme is progressively expanded: personal water, communal water, and global water. In a symbolic sense, water denotes life, so here the scope of life is expanded as such.

rooted in her tradition and she is very proud of it. She is proud of Jacob's well and his religion. Yet this woman does not waste an opportunity for the gift of abundant life offered by Jesus. Jesus' offering of "a spring of water" is reminiscent of Jeremiah's admonition that Jews seek God, "the fountain of living water" (Jer 2:13; 17:13). What Jesus means here is that all people, Jews or Gentiles, have to turn to God, the source of life.[85] But this woman does not understand what Jesus offers or means, saying, "Sir, give me this water, that I may not thirst, nor come here to draw" (4:15). The conversation then moves to the next level, the communal dimension, because such living water should also be available to her village people.

Communal Water (4:16–26)

"Communal water" is a metaphor that stands for communal life in God. Whereas John 4:15 states the need of the woman's personal water ("I may not thirst"), John 4:16 makes a shift to the topic of family. Jesus asks, "Go, call your husband" (v. 17). The woman's response is very surprising since she says, "I have no husband" (v. 17). This woman's answer rings a dire social situation where she has to live without a spouse. Though we are not told what caused her to live without a spouse, we can imagine the difficulties of her life. Jesus supports her by saying that "you are right in saying, 'I have no husband'" (vv. 17–18). After this, topics of conversation include broader community issues such as religion, nation, and the place of worship. Jesus makes clear that all people truly worship God everywhere apart from ethnic origins and places ("worship the Father in spirit and truth," 4:23).

85. Schottroff, "The Samaritan Woman." Schottroff reads the Fourth Gospel and the story of the Samaritan woman as a story of loving relationships that involves God, Jesus, and believers. Jesus leads people to the source of life, which is in God. She says, "I believe that the Fourth Gospel regards not only Jesus but also believers as the source of life for others (4:14). . . The body of Jesus and the bodies of believers are the places of God's new creation and of a loving union" (179–80).

Global Water (4:39–42)

"Global water" is a metaphor that stands for the global significance of life for all because the whole world is the object of God's love. Although "the world" in the Fourth Gospel often conveys negative connotations such as the place of evil (7:7; 14:22, 27; 15:18–19; 16:33; 17:16), it mainly refers to inhabitants on earth. The global significance of the savior is confessed through the village people: Jesus is the savior of the world. What we see here is that the mission of the Logos is more than personal or regional but global, not in the sense of controlling others but in the sense of loving them, as God so loved the world. So the Logos as living water is for all.

The Logos as the Bread of Life (6:22–71)

The bread of life is a metaphor that stands for abundant, holistic life rooted in God, the source of life. After the story of feeding and Jesus' walking on water, Jesus talks about the bread from heaven because the crowds are so slow in understanding his work for God. Jesus says they follow him not because they saw great signs of God but because they ate the loaves of bread. People only saw the bread that they needed for the body; but Jesus wants them to see the source of life in God. That is, people should live by honoring and eating heavenly food, which is none other than service and sacrifice for others. To demonstrate this point, Jesus' miracle here begins with a boy's sharing of bread and fish. Jesus thanked God and distributed the bread and fish to the multitudes through his disciples. The point of the lesson is not that God feeds them supernaturally but that God makes things happen through a little service or sacrifice. A boy's voluntary giving of what he had brings the disciples' participation and the results of this service are shared with the crowds. In this context, Jesus talks about the bread of life because the crowds do not understand the importance of sacrifice and service. Jesus says, "Those who eat my flesh and drink my blood abide in me, and I in them. Just as the living Father sent me, and I live because of the Father, so whoever eats me will live because of me" (6:56–57). This must be a radical, difficult teaching of sacrificial theology.[86] His flesh and blood represents a price of God's love, and his disciples need to follow the way of God in Jesus. Jesus lays down his life out of his love for God and the world. Jesus' sacrifice has a salvific moral power that calls for participation of his followers. Eternal life becomes a reality when people live for God like Jesus.

The Logos as the Light for the World (9:1–41)

With the episode of a blind man's healing, readers are told that life without the light is miserable, and therefore the light is another metaphor for abundant life. So the blind man regains his sight precisely because he is also the child of God. Jesus who is sent by God helps him to recover sight so that he may live with the light. On the other hand, the light is also a metaphor that emphasizes spiritual discernment in a hostile, dark world where human tradition or selfish desires block other people from receiving God's true light. Jewish leaders in this story insist that only they are true disciples of Moses. But Jesus says that they are blind precisely because they say they are not blind. What they see is their own rights and narrow interpretation about Mosaic discipleship, and what they do not see is God's radical freedom and love for all. No one can block others from receiving God's life and light. In contrast with the Pharisees, this blind man gives a testimony about God's blessing and the work done by Jesus. He is a humble man, and distinguishes between what he knows and what he does not. He says he does not know whether Jesus is a sinner or where he is from, but he also says, "One thing I know is, that though I was blind, now I see" (9:25). He shares what he experiences: "Here is an astonishing thing! You do not know where he comes from, and yet he opened my eyes" (9:30). Jesus did it so like the wind: "The wind blows where it chooses, and you hear the sound of it, but you do not know where it comes from or where it goes. So it is with everyone who is born of the Spirit" (3:8). Jesus' identity or origin may not be important compared to his work of God. While Jewish leaders boast of their identity based in a particular tradition, Jesus testifies to the

86. Bailey, "John 6," 95–98.

light of God that must shine on the marginalized people outside of the known tradition.

SUFFERING AND GLORY OF THE LOGOS (13:1— 20:31)

But the Logos is not welcomed in the world primarily for two reasons. On the one hand, people fail to see Jesus' works for God. In other words, they look at Jesus' fingers rather than his works of God to which they point. They see Jesus as son of Joseph only, an ordinary person from Galilee. Even if Jesus does great things for God—feeding the five thousand or healing the sick—they only see the benefits that they receive. Jesus embodies God's love and brings the life and light to the world, but people, including Jesus' disciples, fail to see clearly what Jesus does or why he does so. Religious leaders also fail to understand him; they accuse Jesus with the charge of blasphemy because he said he is the Son of God. On the other hand, the Logos is not welcomed or easily accepted in the world because some people hate the Logos because they fear that their evil acts might be exposed (3:20; 7:7; 12:19–20). Jesus is rejected not because he claims he is God (by the way, he never claims such a title) but because he incarnates the Logos that has the price of God's justice or abundant life for all in the world. As long as Jesus journeys with the Logos, he cannot avoid misunderstandings or opposition from people who have to maintain their interests at the expense of others. In the following, we will see examples of the opposed Logos. We will begin with Peter's denial of Jesus.

Peter's Denial (18:13–27)

Even Peter, one of the core disciples, denies Jesus three times out of his fear that he would be arrested and mistreated like Jesus. Peter's denial of Jesus in a narrative flow is shocking to readers because he said earlier that he would not abandon his teacher: "Lord, to whom can we go, you have the words of eternal life? You are the Holy One of God" (6:68–69). Until this time, readers do not know whether Peter

would deny Jesus at all because Jesus names only Judas as a betrayer.[87]
When Jesus tells his disciples that he will stay a little while with them
(13:33), Peter does not know the meaning and implication of his
teacher's *way* and asks Jesus, "Where are you going?" (13:36). Jesus
answers, "Where I am going, you cannot follow me now; but you will
follow afterward" (13:36). Peter swears confidently in response to
him, "Lord, why can I not follow you now? I will lay down my life for
you" (13:37). Then Jesus predicts Peter's denial three times (13:38).
But the story goes on without knowing whether Peter will really
deny Jesus. At the garden where captors come to arrest Jesus, Peter
shows his loyalty to Jesus by striking the high priest's slave, Malchus,
and by cutting off his right ear (18:10). After Jesus was arrested and
taken to Jerusalem, Peter denies him three times: before the woman
guard of the temple, before the slaves and the police, and before the
slave of the high priest. Peter's denial of Jesus is also contrasted with
Jesus' adamant and calm stance despite the high priest's questioning
of him. While Peter warms his body with people, Jesus is questioned
because of his works of God. After the cock crows, Peter fades out in
the narrative until the last chapter when Jesus commissions him after
asking Peter three times: "Do you love me?"

Pilate's Interrogation (18:28–40)

Pilate, the governor of the Roman Empire, represents the imperial
power and control of other people. He bluntly interrogates Jesus,
"Where are you from?" (John 19:9). As for Pilate, the fact that Jesus
comes from the countryside of Galilee is ridiculous because Jesus is
not a power figure or elite in his eyes. But Jesus says that he came to
testify to the truth (of God). But Pilate asks, what is truth? In fact,
Pilate knows the truth is the way of Rome: the rule of Caesar. But this
time Jesus does not answer him; perhaps he does not need to respond
because Pilate is so adamant about his own truth.

---

87. Culpepper, *Anatomy of the Fourth Gospel*, 53–54.

THE LOGOS RE-INCARNATE (21:1–25)

Twists and turns of Jesus' journey with the Logos reach the climax in the Epilogue (chap. 21). Jesus' disciples meet Jesus, the risen Lord, and eat with him at the table beside the Sea of Tiberias. Jesus said to them, "Come and have breakfast" (21:12). "Now none of the disciples dared to ask him, 'Who are you?' because they knew it was the Lord" (21:12). Jesus "took the bread and gave it to them, and did the same with the fish" (21:13). Certainly, his disciples must have remembered his feeding of the multitude in Galilee (6:9–11). At this very moment, his disciples suddenly recognize the risen Lord. Nobody asks, "Who are you?" because they see, feel, touch, and experience the risen Lord. Now with the risen Lord at the seaside the wind blows to remind them of their true identity in the Lord. The disciples are reconciled with Jesus after having fled from him. The farewell meal prepared by the risen Lord is a moment of remembering the earthly ministry of Jesus—his ministry of the Logos and his time of suffering because of the Logos. We can say that the Logos symbolically reincarnates with Jesus' disciples who now understand Jesus and his works for God, including the cost of the Logos. As Jesus incarnates and journeys with it, now his disciples see, eat, touch, and feel the very presence of the Logos in the community. The risen Lord's presence with his disciples embarks a new beginning for them. Before his return to the Father, Jesus appears three times to make sure they continue in his teaching that he works for God.

Only at the third time, toward the end of the narrative, do the disciples feel the presence of Jesus the risen Lord. Here and after the communal meal together, Jesus asks Peter three times, "Do you love me?" Jesus' question to Peter is inviting and mends broken relationships between him and Peter. Jesus commissions Peter as a shepherd who will lay down his life for the sheep. Thus Peter will become an "exemplary disciple" because of his love and sacrifice for the sheep.[88] He continues to take the mission of the Logos as a good shepherd.

88. Culpepper, "Peter as Exemplary Disciple in John 21:15–19," 165–78.

Truth, Testimony, and Transformation

SUMMARY

In this chapter, we have explored how costly the mission of the Logos is. We have also explored Jesus' journey with the Logos. The price of such a journey is huge, resulting in his death on a cross. The Logos journey reaches its peak when the risen Lord meets with his disciples at the seaside of Tiberias. Then Peter is questioned, reaffirmed, and sent for shepherding the flocks. After Jesus' return, the Advocate (*parakletos*) will come on behalf of Jesus to remind them of his teaching. While Jesus returns to the Father, the Logos will continue to live with his disciples. This is a continuation of the Logos reincarnated with his disciples. As the wind blows from nowhere, the Spirit blows endlessly and enriches life in the world.

5

Logic of the Transformation in John 14:6

Symbols or metaphors in the Fourth Gospel speak of "the presence of greater realities"[89] in God's universe. Light, wind, water, and bread characterize an ideal, natural space necessary for humanity.[90] Wind, water, bread, and light are four important symbols or metaphors in nature, which set up an ideal natural space for the human world. Light is the very first element we see in the prologue. Logos brings the light to the world. Light represents the dignity of life, as we see from the blind man episode in John 9. Water is essential for everybody regardless of ethnicity, religion, or gender, as we see from the Samaritan woman episode in John 4. Water also represents the image of abundant life. Interestingly, water also has the image of flexibility and humbling attitude since it adapts to anything and flows to

89. Brodie, *The Gospel According to John*, 17. In the Fourth Gospel, "many forms of contradiction (including shocks, style change, obscurities, riddles, and breaks) may serve as "a constant challenge, an invitation to move beyond superficiality and to enter into a new awareness, ultimately into the level of the holy" (19). See also Culpepper, *Anatomy of the Fourth Gospel*, 180–98.

90. Mary Coloe takes temple as a main symbol in her study of the Fourth Gospel and claims that "many dwelling places in my Father's house" (John 14:2) should be read as "a variety of interpersonal relationships between the Father, Jesus, *Paraclete*, and believers." See Coloe, *God Dwells With Us: Temple Symbolism in the Fourth Gospel*, 162.

lowly places only to provide the world with abundant life. Wind emphasizes a distributive justice for all, as the wind blows everywhere. Interestingly, wind is the same as the Spirit (*ruah*) in Hebrew. Like the wind, the Spirit works for all because all want a fairly free and just life. Likely, bread represents physical and spiritual food for all, which cannot be manipulated by any ideology or human interests.

The ideal symbolic transformative space does not become a reality without engaging in the Logos, as Jesus pithily pinpoints three important elements in the process of engagement in 14:6, "I am the way, the truth, and the life; nobody comes to the Father except through me."[91] The ideal symbolic space can be realized only when a person engages the way, embodies the truth, and emancipates the life entangled with darkness. In the previous section we have seen Jesus' journey with the Logos and have understood how Jesus engages the way of God, embodies the love of God, and emancipates the world of darkness. John 14:6 is at the center of the symbolic, transformative structure in the Fourth Gospel.

THREE STEPS: ENGAGEMENT, EMBODIMENT, AND EMANCIPATION

John 14:6 appears to be unique among the "I am" sayings of Jesus since three metaphors (the way, the truth, and the life) are combined in one verse. In this section, we will see more closely how John 14:6 functions as the logic of transformation. It has three movements within it: engaging the way, embodying the truth, and emancipating the life.[92] At times people do not know the way, and at other times

91. The Synoptic Gospels also talk about the way, the truth, and the life. Matthew's Gospel talks about *the way*, which is "the *difficult* way and the '*way of righteousness*' (Matt 7:14; 21:28–32) that leads to life." Similarly, Anderson goes on to observe: "The way of God in *truth* is what Jesus teaches in the Synoptic Gospels (Matt 22:16; Mark 12:14, 32; Luke 20:21)"; "the narrow way leads to life (Matt 7:14), and Jesus discusses what it means to inherit *eternal life* (Matt 19:16, 23–30; 10:17; Mark 10:23–31; Luke 18:18, 24–30)." See Anderson, "The Origin and Development of the Johannine *Ego Eimi*," 25.

92. Alan Culpepper states: "In John 14:6, Jesus declares that he is 'the way, the truth, and the life,' that is, *the process, the goal, and the result*" (italics are mine). In some sense, his idea is very close to mine because we know from Jesus how he engages the way (the process), how he testifies to the truth of God (the

they do not like to live the truth. As a result, their lives are darkened, enslaved by worldly desires. Before looking at these three steps, we first need to explore the meaning or concept of the way, the truth, and the life in 14:6.

"The way" (*hodos*) in the Hebrew Bible primarily refers to the way of God. For example, "Teach me your way, O Lord, that I may walk in truth; give me an undivided heart to revere your name" (Ps 86:11; cf. Ps 27:11). The way of God has to do with following "the law of the Lord" (Ps 1:2), which means God's sovereignty, love, promise, and justice. Similarly, Amos urges people to seek the Lord and live (Amos 5:1-17). Since the Fourth Gospel is a very Jewish version of the good news, it is not difficult to reason that the concept of the way in John 14:6 is closer to the Hebrew Bible (see, for instance, Jer 5:4) than to the Gnostic or Hellenistic concept.[93] Jesus seeks God's will and discerns the way of God. In the narrative of the Fourth Gospel, we can trace the path of Jesus' life rooted in the way of the cross (laying down his life for others)—a way of life shown in Jesus' mission work called the Logos mission.[94]

As we read the Fourth Gospel, the way of God is not discerned or understood by people, including Jesus' disciples. The way for Pilate is the way of the Roman Empire, and the way for Jewish leaders is the strict observance of the Mosaic Law ("We are Moses' disciples"; 9:28). The way for other Jewish elites could be the Jerusalem Temple. The way for the Qumran community may be special teachings of the community leader. But the way for the Johannine community is the way of God shown and testified by Jesus as the Jewish Messiah, who lays down his life for others.[95] Here I dissent from Raymond

---

goal), and how he works hard to set free the people (the result of his work). See Culpepper, "Realized Eschatology in the Experience of the Johannine Community," 257. See also Hull, *John*, 334.

93. Brown, *John*, lii–lxiv. The Greek word *hodos* (way) symbolically refers to "a way of life, a practice" (Smith, *John*, 268). For example: "the way of wisdom" (Prov 4:11; "the way of the Lord" in Jer 5:4).

94. See Isa 40:3: "Make straight the way of the Lord." John the Baptist proclaims it before Jesus. Jesus also continues proclaiming and living for the way of the Lord.

95. The Synoptic Gospels also emphasize a similar notion of the way of God. In Matt 21:28-32 Jesus mentions "the way of righteousness" and similarly, in 7:13-14, Jesus asks to enter the narrow gate. Echoing Isa 40:3, John the

Truth, Testimony, and Transformation

Brown and other scholars who suggest that the way for the Johannine community is Jesus who replaces the Temple. Jesus does not attempt to destroy the Temple although he cleanses it. Jesus' act of temple cleansing is a symbolic act signifying that God must be the center of the Temple. His gesture is much like a prophetic act for God's justice. Moreover, Jesus does not replace the kingdom of God, a major theme of the Synoptic Gospels, with something else, as if he were not interested in the reign of God. In the Fourth Gospel, Jesus came to witness to the way of God, embodying God's presence or Logos in the world so that people may live abundantly in the reign of God.

Second, "the truth" (*aletheia*) also basically refers to the character of God. God is true because God's way is not only discernible but also enlightening to the world. God is true because things we see are the work of God. God is true because there is no discrimination or inequality with God. This is what the Hebrew concept of truth (*emet*) means: "to be firm or solid."[96] Accordingly, the truth cannot be separate from the way, as in Psalm 86:11: "Teach me your way, O Lord, that I may walk in truth; give me an undivided heart to revere your name." The way and truth are like two sides of a coin. Once the way of God is discerned, it must be acted out in all spheres of life, which is the life in truth. With this line of thought, the truth in John 14:6 means Jesus' testimony about the way of God so that people may know God is true not merely because he is perfect but because God acts out his love and justice in the world.[97] In his regard, the concept of truth is close to the Hebrew noun, *hesed*, which means God's steadfast love. The one who acts out the truth of God is Jesus, the Son of God, sent by God the Father. Jesus stands for the truth of God on behalf of people because they dwell in darkness, being oppressed under the power of evil. What matters is a testimony to the costly truth

---

Baptist comes to prepare "the way" for the Messiah (Matt 3:3; Mark 1:3; Luke 3:3–4; John 1:23).

96. Brown, *John*, 1:499.

97. Otherwise, the concept of truth in the Fourth Gospel does not come from the Hellenistic philosophy, particularly from a Platonic concept of dualism between ultimate reality and shadow. Jesus as the Jewish Messiah works for God to testify to the truth of God. In other words, Jesus himself is not the truth apart from God's way.

that all are equal and dignified before God.[98] That is where we hear Jesus underscoring the faithful keeping of his teaching, by which the truth will be known.

Third, "the life" (*zoe*) also concerns the character of God in the Hebrew Bible. God is the source of life and light as we see in Genesis. God chooses people to make a light for others in the world so that all may live abundantly. God sends Moses to deliver Israelites out of bondage in Egypt. True life is a continual theme in the major narrative of the Hebrew Bible. That same theme continues in the Fourth Gospel, as John 20:31 clearly states the purpose of writing the Fourth Gospel: "So that you may come to believe that Jesus is the Messiah, the Son of God, and that through believing you may have life in his name." Jesus as the Messiah does the work of God to bring the life and the light to the world. That is his job stated in the prologue of the Gospel. True life means a person's quality relationship with God, following the way of God in truth. That is what the Fourth Gospel refers to as "eternal life."[99]

Engage the Way

Taking together all these concepts of the way, the truth, and the life in John 14:6, we now explore three steps of transformation.[100] The first

98. In the Synoptic Gospels also, there is a similar notion of the truth; for example, Jesus teaches "the way of God in accordance with truth" (Matt 22:16; Mark 12:14; Luke 21), which means his testimony to God's way that entails oppositions or persecutions from those who resist the way and the truth of God.

99. In the Synoptic Gospels there is a similar notion of life or eternal life. For example, the narrow gate leads to life (Matt 7:14), and to inherit eternal life one must serve the poor or the least (Matt 19:16; Mark 10:17; Luke 18:18). In all of these references, eternal life is an ongoing expression of what things are done for the kingdom of God.

100. Interestingly, John 8:30–31 also contains similar notions of a three-step transformation: "If you continue in my word, you are truly my disciples; and you will know the truth, and the truth will make you free." The phrase "continuing in my word" has to do with engaging (discerning) the way because a person has to know what is the way. As a result, he or she will "know the truth," which requires a life of embodying or testifying to the truth. Then, freedom comes: "the truth will make you free," which is the ongoing state of eternal life. We see here the three steps of transformation: discerning the way (engagement), giving testimony to the truth (embodiment), and freeing the life (emancipation).

step is a cognitive level in which a person should ask why he or she takes certain actions. Important questions are: What is the way that Jesus talks about?[101] In what sense is he the way? How does Jesus respond to the way? What are some difficulties or obstacles lying before the way? These questions involve engaging the way or discernment of it: How can we live and for what? Actually in the Fourth Gospel we see a full range of this level of engagement. In the following we will see some of these examples.

The Way and Nicodemus

Nicodemus comes to Jesus to engage or discern the way, but we see how difficult it is for him to understand the way of which Jesus talks. Whereas Jesus talks about the way of God—the life of spiritual birth from above—Nicodemus thinks of it in terms of a physical birth. But the birth or the way of life that Jesus talks about is metaphorical; Jesus talks about a spiritual birth that involves a constant renewal of the person through a continuous relationship with the Spirit. As long as a person maintains such a relationship with God, he or she lives in it. That is what eternal life means in the Fourth Gospel.[102]

Nicodemus's confidence about his tradition blocks him from seeing the work of God, which can happen with anyone, even outside of the traditional Mosaic box. Now Jesus helps him to find a way to resolve his cognitive dissonance. Jesus' point is that one's identity or social position does not necessarily produce good works. That is, there is no guarantee that one's identity coheres with his or her work. God's works can be done by anybody. So Jesus explains this truth,

101. "The way" (*hodos*) in the Fourth Gospel is primarily the way of the Lord (Isa 40:3; John 1:23). Isaiah's vision of the future kingdom of Israel is based on justice, peace, and love. Moses led the Israelites out of Egypt because God made the way out. The way of God is liberation for God's people. In this light, when Jesus says "I am the way," it means he shows the way of God (Isa 40:3), the way of righteousness and justice. His living of the way requires a cost because it is a difficult road. People reject the Logos mission of Jesus. Jesus incarnates the Logos through his life-way.

102. Culpepper, "Realized Eschatology in the Experience of the Johannine Community," 257. Culpepper's statement about eternal life is worth stating here: "Eternal life, therefore, is the present experience of the believer who lives in the knowledge and fellowship of God through the revelation of Jesus."

using an analogy of the wind. That is, a spiritual person is the one who blows like the wind.

The Way and a Samaritan Woman

A Samaritan woman also engages with Jesus about the way of life and finds that God loves all regardless of race, religion, or gender. Initially, Jesus crosses a social religious boundary by asking her for a drink since a Jewish man cannot talk to a foreign woman. But she is not shy and asks him: "How is it that you, a Jew, ask a drink of me, a woman of Samaria?" Now this woman also crosses her social convention that she is not supposed to talk with a Jewish man. But she engages him by asking questions. Gradually, her understanding about him is deepened, and their conversation is moving to a higher level that involves worship place, messiah, and the role of religion. What she finds is the way of God who loves all and the way of Jesus who incarnates the love of God.

The Way and Jesus' Disciples

Thomas says: "Lord, we do not know where you are going. How can we know the way?" Thomas thinks of the way in terms of Jesus' going somewhere in a similar way to Nicodemus thinking of birth as only physical. Jesus shows the way of God to the disciples and people in the world, but they do not understand. But still people think of the way as a place to go, and they do not see the way of God manifest in Jesus' work.

Embody the Truth

As a result of engaging the way of God, there must be a life of testimony to the truth that God is love and justice for all in the world. Here the truth does not mean a set of teaching or doctrine but an ongoing life engaging activities because of the truth of God.[103] In

103. "The truth" (*aletheia*) in the Fourth Gospel is not different from the Synoptic Gospels, as "the way of God in truth is what Jesus teaches (Matt

other words, the truth has to do with God's sovereignty, God's initiative of love, and consequential human dignity attached to it. But embodiment of the truth is difficult because there is a cost of living the truth. It is like the ancient prophets who speak and testify to God's word. Amos speaks God's word of judgment, and because of that, a royal priest, Amaziah, resists him. Jeremiah has difficulties because he speaks the word of God in Jerusalem, but he is resisted because he spoke the word of God, the way of God. The Beloved Disciple testifies to the truth. In the epilogue (John 21), he is told by Jesus that he should remain to lead a community of faith, whereas Peter, after being restored to his relationship with the risen Lord, is told that he will die as a martyr for Christ. Both figures are expected in the future to testify to the truth of God and Jesus' work of God.

Emancipate the Life

The ultimate goal of transformation is a life of freedom and empowerment.[104] The point is that transformation is not a static result, accomplished once and for all. The goal is freedom, not an excessive individualistic freedom but the freedom to share with others. Individualistic, excessive freedom seekers are shunned in the Fourth Gospel. Responsible freedom for public goods and the whole world must be the goal of transformation that brings back the abundant life of Eden.[105] This goal is achieved through a continual, ongoing

---

22:16; Mark 12:14, 32; Luke 20:21). Similarly, in the Fourth Gospel "the truth is liberating, Jesus speaks the truth, and Jesus embodies the truth (John 8:32; 10:45–46; 14:6). See Anderson, "The Origin and Development of the Johannine *Ego Eimi*," 25.

104. "The life" (*zoe*) in the Fourth Gospel is not different from the Synoptic Gospels, as Paul Anderson observes: "The narrow way leads to life (Matt 7:14), and Jesus discusses what it means to inherit *eternal life* (Matt 19:16, 23–30; 10:17; Mark 10:23–31; Luke 18:18, 24–30)." Similarly, in the Fourth Gospel, life comes effective to believers when they engage the difficult way and testify to the truth, like Jesus the Logos incarnate (John 3:15–16, 36; 10:10; 11:25; 14:6; 17:2–3). See Anderson, "The Origin and Development of the Johannine *Ego Eimi*," 25.

105. Robert Bellah issues a warning about a naïve reading of religious language: "The mistake arises when we take language which is deeply contextual, that is confessional, and in the case of Paul probably also liturgical, and turn it into objective assertions of a quasi-scientific form that give us information

commitment to the truth of God. "If you continue in my word, you are truly my disciples; and you will know the truth, and the truth will make you free" (John 8:32). True discipleship is conditional, and disciples continually have to follow the way of life with Jesus. Disciple-making is not done at one time. Notice the conditional clause, "If you continue in my word." Here "my word" is the word and action of Jesus to embody the truth. In order to keep Jesus' word, disciples continually have to discern the way of God with Jesus. Then they will know the truth of God as we saw earlier. Here knowing the truth is not a static knowledge but the embodied truth. As a result of embodying the truth, it will make them free. We notice here, as well, the future tense. Freedom is not gained or achieved by one-time embodiment. Rather, it is the result of a life of ongoing transformation through discernment of the way and embodiment of the truth.

SUMMARY

In this chapter, we have explored a symbolic transformative space, the steps of transformation, and especially the three steps of transformation in John 14:6 and 8:31–32. Those who follow Jesus' work of God are called the children of God (1:12), dwelling in the light, living the life fully through Jesus (20:31). If one believes that Jesus is the Messiah sent by God and continues to remain in Jesus' teaching and life of the Logos, he or she becomes a child of God. Power to become children of God is not based solely on Jesus' death as if he came to die for sinners once and for all. The idea of substitutionary death is Caiaphas's as he suggests that Jesus be put to death for the people of Israel to avoid Roman suppression (18:14). In the Fourth Gospel, believing in Jesus involves acknowledging God the Father who has sent Jesus to liberate the world from the darkness. Such believing requires believers to participate in the mission of the Logos initiated by Jesus.

---

about the eternal fate of non-Christians." See Bellah, "At Home and Not at Home," 425. Therefore, the truth should be engaged in a community in which one lives, embodied in a world beyond one's immediate community, and testified at all costs because of the love of God for all. Truth is not possessive, but requires a life that engages the way, the truth, and the life as we get clues from John 14:6.

6

Transformation in the Fourth Gospel and the Johannine Community

The Fourth Gospel reveals the source of transformation for the Johannine community by narrating the way Jesus teaches and acts out the way of transformation: inviting people to live in the light, changing self-centered lives to Logos-centered lives, and overcoming dualism between "us and them."[106] The Johannine community is supposed to follow the Johannine story and be motivated and challenged to live like Jesus the Jewish Messiah (and the Son of God), who transgresses boundaries because of the love of God for all.[107] In

106. In a sociological approach, the Johannine community is viewed as sectarian. Likewise, high Christology or dualistic language is understood as supporting such an ideology of separation and protecting isolated members from the harsh treatment of the mainline community (legitimation theory). See Meeks, "The Man from Heaven in Johannine Sectarianism," 44–72. Although the sociological approach sheds new light on our understanding of the Johannine community, it certainly has limits, failing to consider the dimension of transformation for the Johannine community.

107. Earlier we saw the "I am" sayings of Jesus are to be understood as part of the larger mission of the Logos embodied by Jesus. Jesus represents God's presence in the world. He is the Son of God sent by God. Jesus incarnates the Logos and shows the way, the truth, and the life of transformation.

a way, the story of the Fourth Gospel is the story of transformation for the community because it fleshes out a new vision of an inclusive community. The Johannine community stretches out to all beyond a small, isolated self-protected community.

In order to see what kind of transformation the community underwent, we have to begin with the Johannine community's most difficult experience: its separation and expulsion from the synagogue, because the experience of "nothingness" can be a moment of transformation.[108] "Transformation through nothingness" is a starting point for the Johannine community's own transformation.

TRANSFORMATION IN THE FOURTH GOSPEL AND THE JOHANNINE COMMUNITY

It seems clear that this community goes through extreme emotional difficulties due to the religious conflict with the synagogue. It is believed that, initially, the followers of Jesus have a verbal conflict with the fellow members of the synagogue, but eventually they are expelled from the synagogue because of their ardent faith about the Messiah. This expulsion brings forward a sense of bitterness, threat, loss of self, or confusion of identity. Furthermore, it is also believed that these followers of Jesus, living on the threshold of a major city of the Roman Empire, are put under duress within and from the imperial system. Therefore there seems a double marginalization for them: religious separation and social marginalization.

The Psychotheological Aspects of Transformation in the Fourth Gospel

From this double marginality, it is not difficult to find moments of "I am no-one" in this community: expulsion from the synagogue (three times) and Jesus' warning about persecution in his farewell discourse in chapters 16–17. Jesus in the Fourth Gospel encourages and comforts the Johannine Christians. His advice is to stay in the faith, being united with each other. In addition, Jesus also promises

---

108. See more on this theory of transformation in Kim, *A Transformative Reading of the Bible*, esp. 22–38.

the coming of the Advocate (*parakletos*) to them. Jesus' prayer for them, particularly John 17:15–18, shows the necessary encouragement in such a time of crisis:

> I am not asking you to take them out of the world, but I ask you to protect them from the evil one. They do not belong to the world, just as I do not belong to the world. Sanctify them in the truth; your word is truth. As you have sent me into the world, so I have sent them into the world.

The community goes through moments of "I am no-one" or "nothingness" because of its separation and marginalization from the synagogue and society. In a narrative flow, perhaps a man born blind typifies a prime example of "I am no-one." He is treated as no-one because blindness is the result of sin from the perspective of Jewish society.

But these moments of "I am no-one" are not the last of the story, but rather part of the fuller story of human transformation conveyed in the Fourth Gospel. The members of the Johannine community consider separation from the synagogue and the consequent difficulties as the cost of following Jesus. Jesus also knows that the world hates his disciples because of their abiding in God through the Son. Thus Jesus prays that God will protect them from evil. We should recognize here Jesus' prayer does not ask God to take them out of the world, in order to deliver them up to heaven out of their painful "nothingness" experience. What matters is how to overcome their bitterness or nothingness experience with the promise of the Advocate.

This promise of God's presence through the Advocate creates the sense of "I am some-one." They are more than what they are now. A man born blind is more than what he is now. He is also a child of God. Moses' disciples cannot block him from seeing the light of God. A new person of God is born not by human tradition, but based on who God is, the God of all, the God of life and light to all. A Samaritan woman at Jacob's well thought that she was no-one; but now she finds a new identity in God through the Messiah. She becomes someone special. Paradoxically from the Fourth Gospel's perspective, while Pilate thinks he is special, he is indeed miserable.

The sense of "I am some-one" is not the goal of transformation. The next step of "I am one-for-others" furthers the process of transformation. In the last chapter of the Fourth Gospel, we see an example of the three-mode transformation. Peter and his companions went to the Sea of Tiberias to catch fish because they were at a loss and frustrated by Jesus' death. This is the mode of "I am no-one." But the risen Lord appears to them at sea to restore them to their true place of unity and service for others. This is the beginning of "I am some-one." Eventually, the disciples recognize him not by asking questions or looking at him but by their remembering what they had heard about the gospel and the community. This is a moment of remembering Jesus and the Logos mission, on one the hand, and also re-membering the community based on love and sacrifice, on the other. This is the beginning of "I am one-for-others." Jesus reminds them that his mission is to give abundant life to all; the symbolic gesture for doing this is to break the bread and fish (like his body as sacrifice) and eat them together. The stock images here are sacrifice (bread and fish are cooked) and communion (Jesus and his disciples eat together in a circle). Symbolically, the fellowship table is a demonstration of love, care, and service for the gathered circle. It could be a future table around which many others are invited to participate—a moment of "I am one-for-others." The climax of this mode is shown in Jesus' questions to Peter three times, "Do you love me?" Peter answers yes each time but Jesus answers, "Feed my sheep." The goal of the Logos is to love, to feed sheep, which entails sacrifices.

The Ontological-Theological Aspects of Transformation in the Fourth Gospel

The ontological-theological transformation concerns three modes of human existence—autonomy, relationality, and heteronomy—which constitute the identity of human ethical lives. Namely, while the self-reliant, independent spirit is necessary for an individual, he or she cannot live isolated from the community and cannot be fully satisfied by themselves apart from the wholly Other (God). Similarly, the members of the Johannine community need all three modes kept in balance. They find confidence in their new identity in Christ and recover the sense of who they are in terms of the children of the light. This is the mode of autonomy, a new existence in which there is a sense of a new birth by the Spirit. Jesus talks about spiritual birth in John 3 but the sense of autonomy here involves heteronomy and relationality. What they are now is because of God's love and Christ's love and his voluntary sacrifice for the world. In a way, autonomy cannot stand without God and Jesus. Even Jesus seeks God's will and works for God's mission. He always says that he is sent by God and is doing God's work. That is the heteronomy of Jesus; yet, Jesus does everything voluntarily (autonomy). The spiritual person is free like the blowing wind, and yet he or she should be born from above (*anothen*), which designates the source of freedom, namely God or the Spirit. Therefore, autonomy here is informed by heteronomy, and both are complementary in matters of Christian life. Certainly, the confident Christian identity (autonomy) requires following the Logos of God delivered by Jesus (John 8:31–32). Mere belief in Jesus is hollow if there is no abiding by Jesus' teaching that embodies God's Logos. If they abide by his word, they are truly his disciples. Because of this, they shall be free (notice here this is the future tense). Jesus says, "the truth will make you free" (John 8:32). The truth concerns who God is and how much he loves the world. But truth is not complete unless it is lived out through faithful keeping of God's Logos and Jesus' teaching.

As is clear now, the Johannine community is not self-reliant, living in an isolated community and seeking its own salvation only because the Jewish Messiah keeps telling them that his mission is for the world (John 3:16). The prologue of the Fourth Gospel makes clear that the purpose of the Logos is to bring the light and life to the world where people are busy seeking their own interests. The purpose of the Fourth Gospel is to help the readers believe that Jesus is the Jewish Messiah who shows God's love to the world and who wants people to live abundantly in the light (John 20:31). The focus is relationality in that the Johannine community should be a light to others who dwell in darkness, hoping for the world's transformation in Christ because of the love of God.

The Political-Theological Aspects of Transformation in the Fourth Gospel

The need of political-theological transformation begins with Jesus' imminent departure to the Father (John 17:13–19). In his farewell speech, Jesus says that he "has given them (disciples) your word (the Logos of God), and the world has hated them because they do not belong to the world, just as I do not belong to the world" (John 17:14). What we see here is that there is a hostile relationship between the disciples and the world because of the Logos of God delivered by Jesus. The world hates disciples; however, Jesus does not pray that God "take them out of the world" but that he "protect them from the evil one" (17:15). Jesus' prayer engages in the world: "Sanctify them in the truth; *your word* is truth" (17:17). Note here that the disciples have to be sanctified in the truth because "your word" (God's Logos) is truth. Though Jesus leaves the world now, the disciples have to stay in the world because they have to do the works of God. So Jesus continues to pray to the Father God: "As you have sent me into the world, so I have sent them into the world" (17:18).

As we saw in Jesus' farewell speech in John 17, Jesus wants the disciples (namely the members of the community in this case) to live in the world even in the midst of hatred and persecution because they have to show the world that they are Jesus' disciples, and that the Logos of God is the truth. As Jesus came to testify to the truth, so Jesus sends them to the world. Jesus does not provide them with an escape from the world; rather, they have to live in the world, dealing with people including those who hate the Logos of God. As Jesus has risked his life for the Logos of God, the disciples have to follow the same way of Jesus testifying to the truth. Jesus encourages them to stay with the truth and to the world. This implies that they do not form a separate sectarian community fending off the world. The opposite message is clear because the mission of the Logos shown by Jesus is costly. The purpose of their staying in the faith is clear; they have to do the work of God (as Jesus sends them for that purpose as he was sent by God) by discerning the way, testifying to the truth, and witnessing the liberation of life from darkness.

As we see above, there is an implicit dimension of political-theological transformation in Jesus' farewell speech. Since "the world" is a political term that involves people, politics, religion, and culture, Jesus' speech about the world connotes political and theological messages to his disciples. Namely, they have to testify to the truth of God (theological dimension) in the world (political dimension). The world (enemies or friends) as a whole is a mission field because it is God's. What are the members of the Johannine community supposed to do in a hostile world? The answer is political and theological: while not belonging to the world, they have to work in the world for the truth of God. If we follow this line of thought that they are to testify to the Logos of God in a hostile world, the Johannine Christians are asked to follow a costly track of the Logos. There is no concept of a self-sufficient, isolated sectarian community that does not need the world.

This importance of positive engagement in the world is further shown in Jesus' prayer about unity between the Father, Jesus, and disciples: "They may all be one. As you, Father, are in me and I am in you, may they also be in us, so that *the world* may believe that you have sent me" (17:21). At a surface level, it seems that the Johannine community does not engage in the world because unity is made between God, Jesus, and *disciples* (so that they are one). But at a deeper level, what Jesus prays here is not to ignore or to disengage the world because the world is bad, but to ask the community (or disciples) to engage in the world with God's Logos so that "*the world* may believe that you have sent me" (17:21). The world at large is the mission place and the disciples have to testify to the truth of God in the world. The result is the world at large will be a better place.

Therefore, the purpose of unity stated in 17:21 does not stop at the Johannine community, but it goes beyond it, extending the love of God to the whole world. That is what God wants: "God loves the world" (3:16–17). The Father is the source of love; Jesus is the sender of the Logos (the love of God), giving his flesh for the world (6:33, 51) so that the world may live with the truth (4:42; 12:47). Jesus' unity with the Father is not simply a mutual union between them, but it extends to the unity between him and the community, through which the world may enter into unity with God. Because the world is the scope of the Logos, Jesus sends his disciples to the world to "bear a redemptive witness" (17:18; 20:21).[109] Alan Culpepper notes this kind of community mandate very well: "The community, therefore, maintains its ethical separation from the world, while continuing to seek to be a redemptive, revelatory presence in it."[110]

109. Culpepper, "Realized Eschatology," 275.
110. Ibid.

The point is that the unity here is threefold: the unity between God, Jesus who embodies the Logos, and the world. Jesus' saying of "I am the vine" is a pertinent metaphor that shows this point of the threefold unity. God plants the vine tree in the world, which is God's vineyard. Individuals are branches to the vine tree. People in the world are branches to the vine. Some are attached to it and others are not; that is, some follow the way of the Logos, testifying to the truth and participating in the work of liberation from evil, but others evade the truth—some even persecuting those who live by the truth. Jesus shows the way of God, testifies to the truth, and liberates the life (John 14:6). Through his incarnation of the Logos, people come to the Father.

Also, what this vine metaphor implies is that the world—the vineyard—is the place of bearing fruits. To make that happen, God, Jesus, and the world come together. God alone is not enough; Christ alone is not enough. The world as a whole as God's vineyard must be restored so that it once again comes back to the abundant garden like the Garden of Eden. Because of that global restoration, the Logos of God goes beyond ethnic and traditional boundaries that set people apart from the love of God. The power of the Fourth Gospel challenges a narrow conception of God who takes care of a select few people, and instead it encourages the community to go beyond what they are so that it turns toward being a more inclusive community working for the whole world.

The transformation of the world is the goal of the unity between God and Jesus, because the world as a whole may believe the truth of God.[111] Through the Johannine community, the world may come to the love of God. The vision and mission of the Logos of God, as stated in the prologue, is achieved through the unity of these three parties: God, Jesus, and the world. Jesus is the embodiment of God's love (it is Jesus' identity of I-am). Because of Jesus' embodiment and testimony to the love of God, now followers of Jesus do the same thing. The Logos, beginning with God's creation (John 1:1), is testified through Jesus and his followers up to the end of the world. The Spirit of truth also will join this movement of the Logos.

All this suggests that the unity here is centrifugal because God's love spreads like the light shining on all. This also means that it is

111. Ibid.

impossible to talk about the unity of God and the Christian community by excluding the world because the central circle of God's love moves outward and it is manifested in the world (see Figure 1 below). God's love does not stay with a core group of people, but extends to others. That is how the Logos comes to the world to share God's love in the world. But the irony is, however, that this gift of God's love is not automatically accepted in the world because people love seeking their own power and benefits at the expense of others. In other words, the world that represents evil people or power is centripetal in the sense that it gathers more power and privilege for itself at the expense of others. All riches and powers are accumulated in Rome and with local elites in imperial provinces, but the true love of God in the Fourth Gospel runs in the opposite direction; God wants all to live in peace and justice. That is the purpose of the Logos mentioned in the prologue. But God's love in the world must be testified through the cost, which is like the sacrificial theology that Jesus speaks to in John 6:51–56. In order for the Logos to be effective in the world there must be a life of sacrifice as Jesus demonstrated. Only then can the light shine on the world. As the sun does not choose to shine on particular people, the Logos affects all people. Therefore, the power of the Fourth Gospel is not exclusive to only a few people but participatory in bringing the light and the life to all because the whole world is God's creation.

Figure 1: Unity of God, Jesus, Disciples and the World

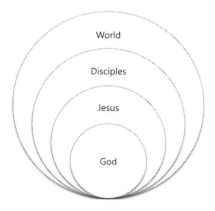

The Cyclic Transformation in the Fourth Gospel

Human transformation is cyclic in nature.[112] Our lives have three moments (attitudes)—*I am no-one, I am some-one, and I am one-for-others*—and all of these moments of life are interdependent and should work together in balance. Transformation is not a linear concept in that one can move from one moment to another in a straightforward line. Rather, these three moments or attitudes of life cycle back and forth, drawing a circle around them.

Interestingly enough, we observe a cycle of transformation in the Fourth Gospel. First, there is a cycle of the Logos: the Logos comes from above, is incarnated with Jesus, re-incarnated with the followers of Jesus after his departure to the Father, and comes back to them through the form of the Advocate (*parakletos*). Interestingly, the beginning and end of the Fourth Gospel is a story about the Logos. In the beginning the Logos comes and in the end the Logos returns. As the wind blows to spread life, as the water flows to deepen life, the work of the Logos done by Jesus helps people to continue to do the work of God by giving testimony to God's giving of life and light to the world. Even though Jesus left the disciples (and the world), the work of the Logos remains with them. The cycle of Jesus' life follows the same path. That is, Jesus comes from God (as the Son of God), embodies the Logos of God, dies in an act of a costly love, is glorified, and returns to the Father. Yet, while Jesus left the world, he still works with people through the work of the Advocate.

Second, there is a cycle of spiritual life. Whereas physical life is linear—from birth to death—spiritual life is cyclic in the sense that it is renewed continually by the power of the Spirit. This is what we have already seen in psychological-theological aspects of transformation that happen through the three moments or attitudes of life. That is, a spiritual person is not born one time as in physical birth; rather, he or she is constantly transformed through the process involving three attitudes of human life (*I am no-one, I am some-one, and I am one-for-others*).

Third, there is also a cycle of events in the Fourth Gospel. For example, as Brodie points out, there are three Passovers in the Fourth Gospel. Symbolically, three Passovers may mean a complexity in

---

112. See Kim, *A Transformative Reading of the Bible*, 66.

65

which issues of life are so entangled that they hardly find easy solutions. Jesus journeys to Jerusalem and back to Galilee for three years. Not surprisingly, the risen Lord appears to the disciples three times to make sure that the love of God is not hollow or a one-time fantasy. The love of God with a new vision should be practiced continually through the rhythm of life. This cyclic Gospel shows us how we (like the Johannine community) should live and die in the world. John's cosmic poetics of the Logos has applicable implications for our lives as we engage the eternal Logos of God in our life journey.[113]

SUMMARY

In this chapter, we have seen how the Johannine community went through different life stages involving moments of separation, joy, and service. The Johannine community's difficult life experience creates a moment of nothingness and at the same time it is a moment of engaging God and the world. Through the experience of nothingness, the community finds the way of God and the way of Jesus. The way of God is the way of love in which the world may live in justice and peace. The way of Jesus is the expression of God's love (or the Logos of God) through his life-risking testimony. The way of the community involves both the way of God and the way of Jesus. Once the community goes through this involvement of the way, it involves a public testimony to the truth of God—the truth that God gives life and light to all in the world.[114]

113. Segovia, "The Journey(s) of the Word of God: A Reading of the Plot of the Fourth Gospel," 23–54.

114. To some degree there is a sense of autonomy because an individual can act on his or her own on the basis of the transformation process: engaging the way, embodying the truth, and emancipating the life. But this degree of autonomy is not self-sufficient because autonomy needs the example of Christ who incarnates the Logos. There is also heteronomy in the sense that God the Father is the source of life and light. There is also relationality because the community should continue the work of God in the world, as we have seen in political/theological transformation.

7

"I Am" Sayings of Jesus in Today's Pluralistic Life Context

Today's life context is full of pluralism that involves all aspects of human life.[115] In deliberation, there are, more or less, three options that we can consider:[116]

115. Alan Culpepper raises similar questions and concerns about the interpretation of the Fourth Gospel: "How should we interpret the theological exclusivism of the Gospel in a pluralistic culture?" (Culpepper, "The Gospel of John as a Document of Faith," 107–27). Culpepper's position seems to be a moderate inclusive leaning. As he writes, "Because the Gospel presents Jesus as the incarnation who made known the work of the Logos from the creation and through all time, it undercuts the triumphalism of claims that Christendom has a monopoly on the revelation of God . . . Just as the Logos brought a saving knowledge of God to Abraham, Moses, and Isaiah, so the Logos continues to speak to persons through other religious traditions as part of God's effort to draw all people to a knowledge of God . . . John's Logos Christology allows Christians to affirm that adherents of other religious traditions may come to know God through the work of the Cosmic Christ" (124). See also Williamson, "Many Rooms, One Way: Preaching John 14 in a Pluralistic Society," 15–20.

116. Lamar Williamson outlines four approaches to the questions of exclusive statement in John 14:6: 1) the text is directed to Jesus' disciples and other religions are not affirmed (exclusive position); 2) Jesus fully reveals God while not rejecting other ways to God or other revelations (mild exclusive position); 3) the cosmic Christ concept that affirms pluralism (pluralistic position); 4) "Accept what this verse affirms about Jesus as the way, truth, and life, but reject what it denies about other approaches to God. Commit to Jesus' way, remain

67

1. The "I am" sayings of Jesus explicitly exclude other religions or people because Jesus is the only way to salvation of humanity.[117]

2. The "I am" sayings of Jesus do not exclude other religions or people because Jesus simply shows the way of God and testifies to the truth of God, which may include works of other religions or activities.

3. The "I am" sayings of Jesus encourage or support a pluralistic position that all religions or truth-claims are relatively true and celebratory in nature.

Option 1 is called "exclusive salvation" against which I have argued in this book. Option 2 is a mild position, neither affirming an exclusive position nor a radical pluralistic position. Option 3 is a pluralistic position that claims all religions are equally valid. While Option 3 seems good to me, in what follows I will explain why Option 2 is a legitimate perspective from the view of the Fourth Gospel and within the context of today's pluralistic society.

CONTEXT OF PLURALISTIC CULTURE

Perhaps nobody can deny that today we live in a pluralistic culture, though not everyone agrees on just what this means. Pluralism or pluralistic culture in general can be understood in several ways. First, there is more diversity of ethnic and religious groups in countries today than in almost any other time in history. America is a good example. While some people are intolerant of this diversity of people, religions, and cultures, others are tolerant about this reality as long as there is no threat to them. It is also true that nowadays many people enjoy or celebrate much about pluralistic cultures: diversity of friendship, music, food, ways of living, patterns of thought, and philosophy.

Second, many countries support the ideal of pluralism in their legal systems. Put differently, pluralism is not a choice that people can make, rather it is given through constitutions or laws. For example,

agnostic about other ways, leaving to God the acceptance or not of their credentials" (inclusive position). See Williamson, *Preaching the Gospel of John: Proclaiming the Living Word*, 182, 313.

117. As part of these sayings, we may include other passages in John since they are seen as exclusive statements by some: John 6:44–45, 53; 15:6.

the U.S. Constitution grants the freedom of speech and the freedom of religion. Diverse cultures, thoughts, and religions can be advocated and promoted under the Constitution.

Third, pluralism is a product of an ongoing intellectual development known as postmodernism. Postmodernism, though divergent in its origins and theories, can be understood as a critical response to reason-based positivistic modernism that tends to push to one grand narrative or universalism (imperialism) at the expense of diversity. When it comes to religion, the gist of postmodernism can be put like this: "No one religion or religious story can represent all about God or the world." In fact, there is a fundamental gap between language and reality. This gap, though unavoidable, speaks to human ideology in that one makes an imaginary or ideal relationship to his or her reality.

In this pluralistic culture, how are we to interpret the "I am" sayings of Jesus? Actually, there are two things involved in this question: our position or interpretation of pluralism and our interpretation of the "I am" sayings in the Fourth Gospel. While some people may see pluralism as a threat to Christianity or faith in general, I want to make the case that such is not the case. Some part of pluralistic thinking may do harm to religious people if relativism is understood as support for irresponsible lifestyle. This could take the form of religious nihilism wherein people think or do anything they like without careful, critical discernment of the way or the truth in relation to others. A more helpful side of pluralism lies rather in the area of epistemology and practical theology. That is, a good question to put to Christians, for example, is, How do we know what is the way or how can we live the way that God wants? While living the truth afresh and appreciating the good part of a cherished tradition, we must be aware of the need of the Spirit that invites us to open our mind and heart to a larger reality we have to embrace.

A common (mis)understanding about the Fourth Gospel, and John 14:6 in particular, is that it opposes pluralism because Jesus is the way, the truth, and the life. But in this book I have explored Logos theology differently than the traditional reading of high Christology. Whereas in the traditional interpretation Jesus is equated with God and the Logos, in this reading Jesus is the Jewish Messiah who embodies the Logos of God. Likewise, the "I am" sayings of Jesus are concrete expressions of the work of God done by Jesus. In other words, what really matters is not Jesus' name but his works for God. In this way, the Fourth Gospel invites all to join with Jesus to do the work of God. Then, surprisingly and suddenly, we realize that this Gospel is very much fitting in the wave of pluralism—a way of living the Spirit most authentically and yet without arrogance or an absolute claim about the truth. In other words, the Fourth Gospel can be very effective within a pluralistic society because it invites readers to engage in the real world without demonizing others. The focus of the Fourth Gospel is not so much directed at non-Christians as at the Johannine community facing double marginality: separation from the synagogue and suppression under Roman control. The Fourth Gospel and the "I am" sayings of Jesus must be understood from this particular historical context where the great needs of the community are a transformation that goes beyond "us-only survival or growth." In other words, the story we read in the Fourth Gospel—a story of the Johannine community—is not a story of triumph like an imperial narrative made out of a violent, victorious war in which others are defeated.[118] Unfortunately, many modern Christians read the Fourth Gospel as a story of triumph and take it with them as a spiritual weapon by which they go out to conquer other non-Christians or other cultures.

That is why I have been so passionate about reading the Fourth Gospel in the context of pluralism. I have lamented the exclusive high Christology not simply because other people or religions are subjugated or subordinated in the name of Jesus or the Logos but because the center or power of the Fourth Gospel has not been realized. The exclusive high Christology rejects local cultures, religions as shown in colonial history. Musa Dube is right when she problematizes from a postcolonial perspective John's colonial conception of

118. Alan Culpepper writes that the Fourth Gospel is fundamentally a story of faith for the oppressed community. See Culpepper, "The Gospel of John as a Document of Faith in a Pluralistic Culture," 107–27. David Rensberger similarly argues the Fourth Gospel is "the product of an oppressed community" (Rensberger, *Johannine Faith and Liberating Community*, 110–32). See also Cassidy, *John's Gospel in New Perspective: Christology and the Realities of Roman Power*, 1. Robert Karris's argument also rings true when he says that both the Johannine community and Jesus were marginalized in the story of Jesus and the community. See Karris, *Jesus and the Marginalized in John's Gospel*, 61.

the otherworldly top-down Logos.[119] As the history of interpretation has shown, the imperial, colonial tendency goes side by side with exclusive Christology.[120] Similarly, eternal life in the Fourth Gospel becomes a means to subjugate other people and religions. The central mode of imperialism or colonialism is based on the superiority of colonizers. Likewise, the Logos also becomes a weapon that rejects all other forms of values, religions, and cultures. Even when Jesus' flesh is emphasized, it is only in the context of his vicarious atonement without consideration of Jesus' ethical life. In a similar vein, John 6:51–56 is often read through the lens of a vicarious death.

This kind of high Christology reading is certainly a predominant one—a position promoted by Western cultures and Christian churches for a long time even up to now. This way of reading actually prevents readers from imitating Jesus as an ethical model. To put it differently, Christians should consider the ethical implication of Jesus' flesh embodiment of the Logos, which should include the very human response of embodying a Christ-like life of forgiveness and self-giving love for others.[121] If Jesus died for us, we also have to die for others because his death is the result of his bold living for God. The implication is that we also need to bear our cross to follow him.[122] In other words, death itself is not the goal of his life.

Because of this kind of moral sacrifice of Jesus in the Fourth Gospel, my reading of the Fourth Gospel is not necessarily exclusive to other cultures or people because, as I stated earlier, Jesus can be understood as the Jewish Messiah who embodies the Logos of God without prejudice against others. Though I agree that the Western reading of the high Christology is problematic, I do not agree that

119. Dube, "Savior of the World but Not of This World: A Postcolonial Interpretation of Spatial Construction in John," 118–35.

120. Faith in Jesus is different from Jesus' faith. Whereas the former has to do with a forensic salvation concept that faith can buy salvation, the latter underscores Jesus' faithfulness that brings God's light and life to the world. Regarding the subject and objective uses of the genitive, see Kim, *A Theological Introduction to Paul's Letters*, 38–108.

121. See especially on this point, Milbank, "The Name of Jesus: Incarnation, Atonement, Ecclesiology," 311–33. See also O'Day, "Jesus as Friend in the Gospel of John," 144–57

122. Howard-Brook, "Reading For/About Our Lives: Politics, Poetics, and Personhood in the Fourth Gospel," 230.

the Fourth Gospel is imperialistic. We can see the transformative power of the Fourth Gospel in God's universal love. This love is not an imperial power; it is a solution to people alienated or separated from their mother community through various forms of oppression.

THE INCLUSIVE, TRANSFORMATIVE CHRISTOLOGY

In this book I have suggested an alternative reading of the Logos. The "I am" sayings of Jesus are expressions and works of the Logos whose goal is to bring the light and life to a hostile, dark world. If my claim is right, there would be no implication of an exclusive salvation to Christians; rather, the point is how to live like Jesus who incarnates the love of God.

The inclusive, transformative Christology is the model for which this book argues. Christ embodies the Logos. The community follows Christ because of his embodiment of God's presence in the world. What matters is participating in God's work through Christ. Various aspects of transformation occur in people and the community. With this model, there is room for a dialogue with other religious people because all in the world can participate in the work of God. Certainly one religion or a particular people do not possess the Logos, but it can be embodied through different people and cultures. Caution should be taken so that this model is not interpreted as promoting a relativism or pluralism in the sense that anything goes. Rather, what matters is an openness to experience a truth deeper than one's tradition. On this matter, it is worth hearing from Herbert Fingarette's *The Self in Transformation*:

> It is the special fate of modern man that he has a "choice" of spiritual visions. The paradox is that although each requires complete commitment for complete validity, we can today generate a context in which we see that no one of them is the sole vision. Thus we must learn to be naïve but undogmatic. That is, we must take the vision as it comes and trust ourselves to it, naively, as reality. Yet we must retain an openness to experience such that the dark shadows deep within one vision are the mute, stubborn

messengers waiting to lead us to a new light and a new vision . . . We must not ignore the fact in this last analysis, commitment to a specific orientation outweighs catholicity of imagery. One may be a sensitive and seasoned journeyer, at ease in many places, but one must have a home. Still, we can be intimate with those we visit, and while we may be only journeyers and guests in some domains, there are our hosts who are truly at home. Home is always home for someone; but there is no Absolute Home in general.[123]

This model of inclusive, transformative Christology also emphasizes "living in truth" for Christians who will follow after Jesus, the one who embodied God's love and testified to it. Therefore, there is no rivalry between Christianity and other religions. Rather, there will be considerable room for engaging in the world for the common goal of peace and justice. Moreover, since this model emphasizes transformation of the self, society, and the world, there will be many opportunities for cooperation and conversations around the topic of transformation.

EXCURSUS: OTHER MODELS OF THE CHRISTOLOGY

Exclusive, High Christology

The view of an exclusive high Christology is a dominant one, familiar to most Christians and non-Christians as well. The simple claim here is that Jesus is God and the preexistent Logos. Jesus' death is the perfect atonement made once and for all by either paying the price of justice for God (satisfaction theory) or being punished in the place of sinners (penal substitution theory). Personal salvation is only through the name of Jesus (so Jesus is the way). Otherwise, there is no emphasis of Jesus' work of the Logos that embodies God's presence in the world. John 14:6 is understood as a definitive statement about the exclusive salvation through

123. Fingarette, *The Self in Transformation*, 236–37.

Jesus who owns the truth and provides the way to heaven. In this high Christology reading, the Christian mission is narrowly understood as spreading the good news about Jesus rather than about God or the Logos that he embodies.

Exclusive, Social Christology

The view of an exclusive, social Christology applies in the Fourth Gospel to a particular community struggling because of its faith in God and in the new Messiah Jesus. This reading has been emphasized through a sociological approach to the Fourth Gospel (for example, in sect theory). Because of the isolated Johannine community's need to survive and grow in the face of opposition and persecution coming from the mother community and the hostile Roman environment, the Gospel tends to be dualistic and exclusivistic so that this new community may feel secure in spite of bitter emotional separation. Within this context, Jesus and his sayings are a salve to the members of the struggling community. The mentality here is "us or them." The language of dualism in the Fourth Gospel is understood through identity struggle and community formation. Otherwise, there is no great emphasis on Jesus' universal or transformative work for God.

Adaptive, Contextual Christology

An adaptive, contextual Christology is understood to be opposed to the exclusive, social Christology. Whereas the latter emphasizes the logic of "us and them" and thus Christ becomes exclusive to the community, the former underscores the internal stability of the community without involving the logic of "us and them." In this model the role of Christ is to provide comfort and legitimation for those who are insecure because of the conflict with the mainline community. But the difference with an exclusive, social Christology is there is no logic of "us and them." This reading of Christology is called adaptive, contextual in the way that the force of the Gospel is directed at members so that they may adapt to a new environment in a particular context of suffering or oppression. The point is that John 14, for example, should be read as a text of comforting these marginalized members of the community. The Logos binds their wounds, heals their souls, and sustains their faith in God through the Messiah Jesus. In this reading, what matters is a particular experience of the marginalized.[124]

CONCLUSION

How can we know who Jesus is without seeing his work of God? If we lose focus on God's work of life and light in the world, our life would be hollow. "I am the way" would be a noisy gong. Who can define what "Christian" means without seeing the work of a Christian? Do we do the work of love, life, and light in this world? Jesus came for that reason and asks his disciples and followers to understand clearly his works: "If I don't do the works of my Father, don't believe me. But if I do them, and you don't believe me, believe the works so that you can know and recognize that the Father is in me and I am in the Father" (John 10:37–38). Jesus makes clear that his mission is to do God's works of life and light in this world. It is the work of the Spirit. It is the work of light and life (9:5). We are also sent to do God's work.

In John 9:1–12 recovery of sight is the main theme. Through God's work, a person now sees a new world, a new life, and a new light. The name of the healing pond is Siloam, which means "sent." Jesus is sent by God to do the work of God. His work is none other than to provide the light and life for all. Who are sons and daughters of God? Jesus says: "Who is my mother and who are my brothers and sisters? They are those who do the will of God." God's work is more important than any other name or tradition. God's thought is above us and surpasses our understanding of any sort. God wants to send ministers to the ponds in which many people await healing. This healing is not an individual, psychological ecstasy that televangelists often offer. The healing is a total awakening of who we are to be in order do God's work in this conflicting tumultuous time.

124. O'Day, *New Interpreter's Study Bible*, 1937.

Truth, Testimony, and Transformation

We must work tirelessly on all aspects of our lives: individual and communal, personal and social, cultural and economic, political and ecological, local and global. In this way the movement is not from identity to work, but rather the reverse. By observing the work of the wind, we only know dimly about the wind. Jesus says the person born of the spirit is like this. The spiritual person does the work of God, aligning with many people around the world who also do the work of God, and all in concert moving like the wind. We have to open our eyes and see the work of others whom God loves and or whom God wants to provide light and life. The task for the followers of Jesus is to continue his work.

We should be known by our work; that is our identity. Sometimes people define others based on their own standards. But we have to declare, "I am more than who I am because I am a person of the spirit. I am more than what others say that I am because I am a person of the spirit. I am known by my work." Like the wind, what matters most is not where one is from but what one does. Do we do the work of the Spirit so that people see God's work in us? Do we do God's work of life and light? What we see is not the wind but the work of the wind.

Like Nicodemus, often we are more concerned about someone's identity based on our prejudices about them. Nicodemus is certainly a learned, respected person in his own community. He knew a lot about his tradition. But because of his own perception of truth, he becomes blind and does not see God's works that take place through Jesus. Today there are also people who are too confident about their own knowledge, which serves as a tool for control and the sacrifice of others' welfare. Often in the name of God or Jesus or in any other name, people block God's works from happening and promote their own ideology and preconceptions. They say they are legitimate people who can do the work of God. God's works are about life and light in the world and go beyond any human standard or tradition. We know Jesus by his work: his giving of life and blood for others. His life of sharing is something that we need to emulate in our own bodies.

Often in Christian theology and ethics, we say, "Become who you are!" You became Christian (status or identity) so you are to live like a Christian (duty). This tends to prioritize identity over ethics. Ethics, I would argue, is not an extension of faith or identity. Christian life cannot be glossed over by any theology or identity. Christian life is ethics, and Christian faith is work by which we represent who we are. Perhaps we have to say it like this: "If I don't live the life of Jesus I am not a Christian any more. If I don't live with the power of the Spirit, I am not a spiritual person any more."

Likewise, in the Fourth Gospel eternal life is not a matter of once-and-for-all possession of the life, nor is it a matter of an afterlife. Often our religiosity exercises too much imagination about the afterlife, which seems to dismiss our humanness. Undeniably, such an imagination downplays the present earthly life that yearns for meaningful resolutions. But Jesus emphasizes his flesh and blood (6:51–56) for us here today. The Word itself became flesh because flesh is essential in this world (1:14). Our primary job is to keep this world safe and peaceful without killing out of hatred or devaluing human life. We need to seek a holiness that binds each person to a greater self, and this bond encompasses all of nature and the world.

Regrettably, many Christians support war in the name of God's justice and peace. In the name of peace they do harm to life. What is wrong with this? Why is human flesh devalued? Can a war be justified when innocent lives are destroyed? It should be mentioned that this earthly physical life even with its finitude embodies sound theology. We have to value life itself whether of humans or animals; all are God's creation. How to value God-given life and to find eternity in our physicality must be the key to the understanding of the Christian message. Likewise, John's vision of the flesh establishes a community of abundant life—all life being cared for (John 10:10–11). This full sense of life involves political, economic, and psychological aspects of abundance.

Arguing against the exclusive reading of John 14:6, I interpret this verse and the Fourth Gospel as a whole as the gospel of love and invitation to all. John 14:6 is a central statement of inclusivism. Moreover, John 14:6 is a key text for holistic human transformation that involves "the way, the truth, and the life." So for the Johannine community the way of God is engaged, the truth of God is testified, and the life is set free. We see Jesus going through this transformation: he discerns the way of God; testifies to the truth; and sets free his life in his crucifixion. Jesus' self-identity is as the one who is sent by God for doing the works of God (4:34; 6:27) through sacrifice and obedience to the will of God. Eating Jesus' flesh and drinking his blood means doing Jesus' work of God as his disciples, embodying God's presence in the world.

As Jesus the Son of God embodies God's presence (the Logos of God) in the world, we continue to testify to the Logos of God, living like the wind—the way of the Spirit. As the wind has no name or origin and yet blows everywhere, the spiritual person is one who freely acts out of God's love and does not discriminate on the basis of race, gender, national origin, religion, marital status, age, disability, or sexual orientation. The spiritual person is not born once, but is constantly renewed by the Spirit from *above (anothen)*. With constant spiritual renewal, let us blow like the wind.

Bibliography

Anderson, Paul. "The Having-Sent-Me Father: Aspects of Agency, Encounter, and Irony in the Johannine Father-Son Relationship." *Semeia* 85 (1999) 33–57.

———. "The Origin and Development of the Johannine *Egō Eimi* Sayings in Cognitive-Critical Perspective." *Journal for the Study of the Historical Jesus* 9 (2011) 139–206.

———. *The Riddles of the Fourth Gospel: An Introduction to John*. Minneapolis: Fortress, 2011.

Arndt, William, F. Wilbur Gingrich, and Walter Bauer, editors. *A Greek-English Lexicon of the New Testament and Other Early Christian Literature*. 2nd ed. Chicago: University of Chicago Press, 1979.

———. *A Greek-English Lexicon of the New Testament and Other Early Christian Literature*. 3rd ed. Chicago: University of Chicago Press, 2000.

Arthur, Rose Hofman. *The Wisdom Goddess: Feminist Motifs in Eight Nag Hammadi Documents*. Lanham, MD: University Press of America, 1984.

Ashton, John. *The Interpretation of John*. London: T. & T. Clark, 1997.

———. *Studying John: Approaches to the Fourth Gospel*. Oxford: Oxford University Press, 1994.

Badiou, Alain. *Saint Paul: The Foundation of Universalism*. Stanford, CA: Stanford University Press, 2003.

Barrett, C. K. *Essays on John*. Philadelphia: Westminster, 1982.

Bailey, Raymond. "John 6." *Review & Expositor* 85/1 (1988) 95–98.

Ball, David. *"I Am" in John's Gospel: Literary Function, Background, and Theological Implications*. JSNTSup 124. Sheffield, UK: Sheffield Academic, 1996.

———. "'My Lord and my God': The Implication of 'I Am' sayings for Religious Pluralism." In *One God, One Lord in a World of Religious Pluralism*, edited by Andrew D. Clarke and Bruce W. Winter, 53–71. London: Tyndale, 1991.

Bellah, Robert. "At Home and Not at Home: Religious Pluralism and Religious Truth." *Christian Century* (April 19, 1995) 423–28.

Borg, Marcus. *Evolution of the Word: The New Testament in the Order the Books Were Written*. New York: HarperOne, 2012.

Bibliography

Bornkamm, Günther. *Jesus of Nazareth*. Minneapolis: Fortress, 1995.

Brodie, Thomas. *The Gospel According to John: A Literary and Theological Commentary*. New York: Oxford University Press, 1993.

Brown, Francis, S. R. Driver, and Charles A. Briggs. *The Brown-Driver-Briggs Hebrew and English Lexicon*. Peabody, MA: Hendrickson: 1995.

Brown, Raymond. *The Gospel According to John*. 2 vols. Garden City, NY: Doubleday, 1980.

Buber, Martin. *Moses: The Revelation and the Covenant*. New York: Humanity, 1998.

Bultmann, Rudolf. *Der zweite Brief an die Korinther*. Göttingen: Vandenhoeck & Ruprecht, 1987.

————. *The Gospel of John*. Translated by G. R. Beasley-Murray. Philadelphia: Westminster, 1971.

————. "The History of Religions Background of the Prologue to the Gospel of John." In *The Interpretation of the Fourth Gospel*, 27–46. Edinburgh: T. & T. Clark, 1997.

————. *The Theology of the New Testament*. 2 vols. New York: Scribner's, 1951–1955.

Carter, Warren. *John and Empire: Initial Explorations*. London: T. & T. Clark, 2008.

Cassidy, R. J. *John's Gospel in New Perspective: Christology and the Realities of Roman Power*. Maryknoll, NY: Orbis, 1992.

Charlesworth, James. "The Dead Scrolls and the Gospel according to John." In *Exploring the Gospel of John*, edited by R. Alan Culpepper and C. Clifton Black, 65–97. Louisville: Westminster John Knox, 1996.

Childs, Brevard. *The Book of Exodus: A Critical, Theological Commentary*. Philadelphia: Westminster, 1974.

Chowdhury, Aniruddha. "Memory, Modernity, Repetition: Walter Benjamin's History." *Telos* 143 (2008) 22–46.

Coloe, Mary L. *God Dwells With Us: Temple Symbolism in the Fourth Gospel*. Collegeville, MN: Liturgical, 2001.

Comfort, P. W. *I Am the Way: A Spiritual Journey through the Gospel of John*. Grand Rapids: Baker, 1994.

Crossan, John Dominic. *The Historical Jesus: The Life of a Mediterranean Jewish Peasant*. New York: HarperCollins, 1992.

Culpepper, R. Alan. *Anatomy of the Fourth Gospel*. Philadelphia: Fortress, 1987.

————. "Cognition in John: The Johannine Signs as Recognition Scenes." *NABPR* 35/3 (2008) 251–60.

————. "Designs for the Church in the Imagery of John 21:1–14." In *Imagery in the Gospel of John: Terms, Forms, Themes, and Theology of Johannine Figurative Language*, edited by Jörg Frey, Jan G. van der Watt, and Ruben Zimmermann, in collaboration with Gabi Kern, 369–402. Tübingen: Mohr/Siebeck 2006.

————. *The Gospel and Letters of John*. Nashville: Abingdon, 1998.

———. "The Gospel of John as a Document of Faith." In *What is John?*, edited by Fernando Segovia, 1:107–27. Atlanta: Scholars, 1998.

———. "Peter as Exemplary Disciple in John 21:15–19." *NABPR* 37/2 (2010) 165–78.

———. "The Pivot of John's Prologue." *NTS* 27 (1981) 1–31.

———. "Realized Eschatology in the Experience of the Johannine Community." In *The Resurrection of Jesus in the Gospel of John*, edited by Craig R. Koester and Reimund Bieringer, 253–76. Tübingen: Mohr/Siebeck, 2008.

Davies, W. D. "Reflections on Aspects of the Jewish Background of the Gospel of John." In *Exploring the Gospel of John*, edited by R. Alan Culpepper and C. Clifton Black, 43–64. Louisville: Westminster John Knox, 1996.

Derrida, Jacques. "Différance." In *Margins of Philosophy*, 1–27. Translated by Alan Bass. Chicago: University of Chicago Press, 1986.

———. "The Villanova Roundtable." In *Deconstruction in a Nutshell: A Conversation with Jacques Derrida*, edited by John Caputo, 1–28. New York: Fordham University Press, 1997.

Dodd, Charles. *The Interpretation of the Fourth Gospel*. Cambridge: Cambridge University Press, 1953.

Dreyfus, Stanley. "The Burning Bush through the Eyes of Midrashi: God's Word Then and Now." In *Preaching Biblical Texts: Expositions by Jewish and Christian Scholars*, edited by Fredrick Carlson Holmgren and Herman E. Schaalman, 62–75. Grand Rapids: Eerdmans, 1995.

Dube, Musa W. "Savior of the World but Not of This World: A Postcolonial Reading of Spatial Construction in John." In *The Postcolonial Bible*, edited by R. S. Sugirtharajah, 118–35. Sheffield: Sheffield Academic, 1998.

Dunn, James D. G. *Did the First Christians Worship Jesus? The New Testament Evidence*. Louisville: Westminster John Knox, 2011.

———. "John and the Oral Gospel Tradition." In *Jesus and the Oral Gospel Tradition*, edited by Henry Wansbrough, 351–79. JSNTSup 64. Sheffield, UK: JSOT Press, 1991.

Feldman, Louis. *Judaism and Hellenism Reconsidered*. Leiden: Brill, 2006.

Fingarette, Herbert. *The Self in Transformation: Psychoanalysis, Philosophy, and the Life of the Spirit*. New York: Basic, 1963.

Fishbane, Michael. *Biblical Text and Texture: A Literary Reading of Selected Texts*. Oxford: Oneworld, 2003.

Freud, Sigmund. *Civilization and Its Discontents*. Translated and edited by James Strachey. New York: Norton, 1961.

Funk, Robert, and Roy Hoover. *The Five Gospels: The Search for the Authentic Words of Jesus: New Translation and Commentary*. New York: Macmillan, 1993.

Gadamer, Hans-Georg. *A Century of Philosophy: A Conversation with Riccardo Dottori*. New York: Continuum, 2006.

Glancy, Jennifer. "Torture: Flesh, Truth, and the Fourth Gospel." *Biblical Interpretation* 13/2 (2005) 107–36.

Bibliography

Harner, P. B. *The "I Am" of the Fourth Gospel: A Study in Johannine Usage and Thought*. Philadelphia: Fortress, 1970.

Hazony, Yoram. *The Philosophy of Hebrew Scripture*. New York: Cambridge University Press, 2012.

Howard-Brook, Wes. "Reading For/About Our Lives: Politics, Poetics, and Personhood in the Fourth Gospel." In *What is John?*, edited by Fernando Segovia, 2:213–30. Atlanta: Scholars, 1998.

Hylen, Susan. *Imperfect Believers: Ambiguous Characters in the Gospel of John*. Louisville: Westminster John Knox, 2009.

Jervis, L. Anne. *At the Heart of the Gospel: Suffering in the Earliest Christian Message*. Grand Rapids: Eerdmans, 2007.

Karris, Robert. *Jesus and the Marginalized in John's Gospel*. Collegeville, MN: Liturgical, 1990.

Käsemann, Ernst. *Essays on New Testament Themes*. Minneapolis: Fortress, 1982.

Kee, Howard. "Aretalogy and Gospel." *Journal of Biblical Literature* 92 (1973) 402–22.

Kim, Yung Suk. *Biblical Interpretation*. Eugene, OR: Pickwick, 2012.

———. *Christ's Body in Corinth*. Minneapolis: Fortress, 2008.

———. *A Theological Introduction to Paul's Letters: Exploring a Threefold Theology of Paul*. Eugene, OR: Cascade, 2011.

Kim, Yung Suk, and Jin-Ho Kim, editors. *Reading Minjung Theology in the Twenty-First Century*. Eugene, OR: Pickwick, 2013.

Kraemer, R. S., editor. *Maenads, Martyrs, Matrons, Monastics: A Sourcebook on Women's Religions in the Greco-Roman World*. Philadelphia: Fortress, 1988.

Kysar, Robert. *John the Maverick Gospel*. Louisville: Westminster John Knox, 1993.

Levenson, Jon. *Sinai and Zion: An Entry into the Jewish Bible*. New York: Harper and Row, 1985.

Levinas, Emmanuel. *Emmanuel Levinas: Basic Philosophical Writings*. Edited by Adriaan T. Peperzak et al. Bloomington: Indiana University Press, 1996.

Martyn, Louis. *History and Theology in the Fourth Gospel*. Louisville: Westminster John Knox, 2003.

Matson, Mark. *John*. Interpretation. Bible Studies. Louisville: Westminster John Knox, 2002.

McCarthy, Dennis. "Exodus 3:14: History, Philosophy and Theology." *CBQ* 40 (1976) 311–22.

McGuire, Anne. "Thunder, Perfect Mind." In *Searching the Scriptures*, , edited by Elizabeth Schüssler Fiorenza, 2:39–54. New York: Crossroad, 1994.

Meeks, Wayne. "The Man from Heaven in Johannine Sectarianism." *JBL* 91/1 (1972) 44–72.

Milbank, John. "The Name of Jesus: Incarnation, Atonement, Ecclesiology." *Modern Theology* 7/4 (1991) 311–33.

Bibliography

Neyrey, J. "'I Am the Door' (John 10.7, 9): Jesus the Broker in the Fourth Gospel." *CBQ* 69 (2007) 271–91.

O'Day, Gail. "Jesus as Friend in the Gospel of John." *Interpretation* 58 (2004) 144–57.

———. "John." In *The New Interpreter's Study Bible*, edited by Walter J. Harrelson, 1905–1951. Nashville: Abingdon, 2003.

Peppard, Michael. *The Son of God in the Roman World: Divine Sonship in its Social and Political Context.* Oxford: Oxford University Press, 2011.

Pereboom, Derk. "Stoic Psychotherapy in Descartes and Spinoza." *Faith and Philosophy* 11 (1994) 592–625.

Reinhard, Kenneth. "Toward a Political Theology of the Neighbor." In *The Neighbor: Three Inquiries in Political Theology*, edited by Slavoj Žižek, Eric Santner et al., 11–75. Chicago: University of Chicago Press, 2005.

Rensberger, David. *Johannine Faith and Liberating Community.* Philadelphia: Westminster, 1988.

———. "Sectarianism and Theological Interpretation in John." In *What is John?*, edited by Fernando Segovia, 2:139–56. Atlanta: Scholars, 1998.

Ricoeur, Paul. *Time and Narrative.* Vol. 3. Translated by by Kathleen McLaughlin and David Pellauer. Chicago: University of Chicago Press, 1988.

Robinson, John. *The Priority of John.* London: SCM, 1985.

Santner, Eric. "Miracles Happen: Benjamin, Rosenzweig, Freud, and the Matter of the Neighbor." In *The Neighbor: Three Inquiries in Political Theology*, edited by Slavoj Zizek et al., 76–133. Chicago: University of Chicago Press, 2005.

———. *On the Psychotheology of Everyday Life: Reflections on Freud and Rosenzweig.* Chicago: University of Chicago Press, 2001.

Schnackenburg, Rudolf. "The Origin and Meaning of the *ego eimi* Formula." Translated by K. Smyth. In *The Gospel According to St. John*, 1:79–89. New York: Seabury, 1980.

Schottroff, Louise. "The Samaritan Woman and the Notion of Sexuality in the Fourth Gospel." In *What is John?*, edited by Fernando Segovia, 2:157–81. Atlanta: SBL, 1998.

Schroer, Silvia. "The Book of Sophia" In *Searching the Scriptures*, edited by Elizabeth Schüssler Fiorenza, 2:17–38. New York: Crossroad, 1994.

Schüssler Fiorenza, Elisabeth. *In Memory of Her: A Feminist Theological Reconstruction of Christian Origins.* New York: Crossroads, 1992.

———. "Wisdom Mythology and the Christological Hymns of the New Testament." In *Aspects of Wisdom in Judaism and Early Christianity*, edited by Robert L. Wilken, 17–41. Notre Dame, IN: Notre Dame University Press, 1975.

Schweizer, Eduard. *Ego Eimi: die religionsgeschichtliche Herkunft und theologische Bedeutung der johanneischen Bildreden, zugleich ein Beitrag zur Quellenfrage des vierten Evangeliums.* Forschungen zur Religion und Literatur des Alten und Neuen Testaments 56. Göttingen: Vandenhoeck & Ruprecht, 1939.

Bibliography

Scott, James. *Domination and the Arts of Resistance: Hidden Transcripts.* New Haven: Yale University Press, 1990.

Scott, Martin. *Sophia and the Johannine Jesus.* JSNTSup 71. Sheffield, UK: Sheffield Academic, 1992.

Segovia, Fernando. "The Journey(s) of the Word of God: A Reading of the Plot of the Fourth Gospel." *Semeia* 53 (1991) 23–54.

Smith, D. M. *The Composition and Order of the Fourth Gospel: Bultmann's Literary Theory.* New Haven: Yale University Press, 1965.

———. *John.* Abingdon New Testament Commentaries. Nashville: Abingdon, 1999.

Smith, Morton. "Prolegomena to a Discussion of Aretalogies, Divine Men, the Gospels, and Jesus." *Journal of Biblical Literature* 90 (1971) 174–99.

Soulen, Richard, and Kendall Soulen. *Handbook of Biblical Criticism.* Louisville: Westminster John Knox, 2001.

Stauffer, Ethelbert. *Jesus and His Story.* New York: Knopf, 1960.

Stibbe, Mark. *John.* Sheffield, UK: Sheffield Academic, 1996.

Temple, William. *Readings in St. John's Gospel.* First Series. London: Macmillan, 1940.

Thompson, Marianne Meye. "The Historical Jesus and the Johannine Christ." In *Exploring the Gospel of John,* edited by R. Alan Culpepper and C. Clifton Black, 21–42. Louisville: Westminster John Knox, 1996.

Trombley, Frank. "Prolegomena to the Systemic Analysis of Late Hellenistic Religion: The Case of the Aretalogy of Isis at Kyme." In *Religious Writings and Religious Systems,* edited by J. Neusner et al., 95–113. Atlanta: Scholars, 1989.

Vassiliadis, Petros. "John in an Orthodox Perspective." In *Global Bible Commentary,* edited by Daniel Patte, 412–18. Nashville: Abingdon, 2004.

Wainwright, Elaine. "Jesus Sophia: An Image Obscured in the Johannine Prologue." *Bible Today* 36/2 (1988) 92–97.

Welborn, Laurence L. "Extraction from the Mortal Site: Badiou on the Resurrection in Paul." *NTS* 55/3 (2009) 295–314.

———. "Paul and Pain: Paul's Emotional Therapy in 2 Corinthians 1.1–2.13; 7.5–16 in the Context of Ancient Psychagogic Literature." *New Testament Studies* 57/4 (2011) 547–70.

Welch, Sharon D. *A Feminist Ethic of Risk.* Minneapolis: Fortress, 1990.

Whitters, Mark. "Discipleship in John: Four Profiles." *Word and World* 18/4 (1998) 422–27.

Williams, C. H. "I Am He." In *Jesus in Johannine Tradition,* edited by R. T. Fortna and T. Thatcher, 16–54. Louisville: Westminster John Knox, 2001.

———. *"I Am He": The Meaning and Interpretation of "ANI HU" in Jewish and Early Christian Literature.* Tübingen: Mohr/Siebeck, 1999.

———. "'I Am' or 'I Am He'? Self-Declaratory Pronouncements in the Fourth Gospel and in the Rabbinic Tradition." In *Jesus in Johannine Tradition,* edited by R. T. Fortna and T. Thatcher, 343–52. Louisville: Westminster John Knox, 2001.

Williamson, Lamar. "Many Rooms, One Way: Preaching John 14 in a Pluralistic Society." *Journal for Preachers* 29/4 (2006) 15–20.

———. *Preaching the Gospel of John: Proclaiming the Living Word.* Louisville: Westminster John Knox, 2004.

Wimberly, Edward P. *Prayer in Pastoral Counseling: Suffering, Healing, and Discernment.* Louisville: Westminster John Knox, 1990.

Yamaguchi, Satoko. "'I Am' Sayings and Women in Context." In *A Feminist Companion to John,* edited by Amy-Jill Levine, 35–40. Sheffield, UK: Sheffield Academic, 2003.

Index

Index

Index

prologue, 2n5, 5, 10, 33, 35, 37, 47,
   51, 60, 63–64
prophetic formula, 18
protection, 9, 17
proskuneo, 2n7
psychotheological, 57

Qumran, 39n82, 49

Rabbi, 3n8, 9n27
race, 53, 78
relationality, 59–60, 66n114
relativism, 69, 72
Res Gestae, 20
Rensberger, David, 70n118
resurrection, 2n4, 30, 32
Robinson, John, 2n6

sacrifice, 5, 41–42, 45, 59–60, 64,
   71, 76–77
sacrificial love, 5
salvific, 6, 42
Samaritan woman, 37–40, 47, 53,
   58
sarx, 36
Schottroff, Louise, 38n79, 40n85
Schroer, Silvia, 19n46
Schüssler Fiorenza, Elisabeth,
   14n34, 19n46
Scott, James, 26n63
Scott, Martin, 14n34, 19n46
sectarian, 56n106, 61–62
Segovia, Fernando, 66n113
Septuagint, 4n12, 15, 36
shub, 19
Smith, D. M., 8n22, 25n56, 49n93
Smith, Morton, 20n47
social beings, 9
social-scientific, 23n52
Society of Biblical Literature, 9,
   24n55
sociological, 9, 56n106, 74
Son of God, 12–13, 19, 27–28, 34,
   43, 50–51, 56, 65, 78
Son of Man, 1n3

space, 13, 21, 47–8, 55
spiritual, 8, 23, 25, 38–39, 42, 48,
   52–53, 59–60, 65, 70, 72,
   76–78
survival, 9, 12, 26, 70
symbolic, 2n4, 10–11, 13, 21,
   39n84, 48, 50, 55, 59
synagogue, 9–10, 24, 26–7, 57–58,
   70
Synoptic Gospels, 7–9, 22–24,
   32n66, 48n91, 49n95, 50–55

Temple, 24, 29, 49–50
Temple, William, 7n21
testimony, 25, 29, 35, 42, 50–53,
   63, 65–66
Thompson, Marianne Meye,
   24n54
Torah, 39n82
triumphalism, 67n115
Trombley, Frank, 20n48
transformation, 9–17, 26–28,
   48–70
tropological, 10
true vine, 2n4, 32
Tiberias, 30, 45–46, 59

union, 8, 62
universalism, 69

Vassiliadis, Petros, 8n24
vicarious death, 5–6, 8, 71
vineyard, 63

Wainwright, Elaine, 14n34
way of God, 2–4, 42, 48–50
Whitters, Mark, 7n19
wilderness, 4, 16–17, 38
Williams, C. H., 18n43
Williamson, Lamar, 67n115
world (*cosmos*), 4n11

Yamaguchi, Satoko, 2n6

zoe, 36, 51, 54n104

Made in the USA
Las Vegas, NV
16 March 2022

45798603R00060